Little Seed Publishing
Laguna Beach, CA

Pre-press Management by New Caledonian Press
Text Design: Angie Kimbro

Cover Design and Illustrations: K-Squared Designs, LLC, www.k2ds.com
Publisher intends this material for entertainment and no legal, medical or other professional advice is implied or expressed. If the purchaser cannot abide by this statement, please return the book for a full refund.

Acknowledgement is made for permission to quote copyrighted materials.

Publisher acknowledges that certain chapters were originally published in similar or identical form in other *Wake Up...Live the Life You Love* books and reprinted by permission of Little Seed Publishing, with all rights reserved.

For information, contact Little Seed Publishing's operations office at Global Partnership: P.O. Box 894, Murray, KY 42071, or phone 270-753-5225 (CST).

Distributed by Global Partnership, LLC
P.O. Box 894
Murray, KY 42071

Library of Congress Cataloguing in Publication Data
Wake Up...Live the Life You Love: Empowered
ISBN-13: 978-1-933063-14-0

$14.95 USA $14.95 Canada

Other books by Steven E, and Lee Beard

Wake Up…Live the Life You Love:
…First Edition
…Second Edition
…Inspirational How-to Stories
…In Beauty
…Living on Purpose
…Finding Your Life's Passion
…Purpose, Passion, Abundance
…Finding Personal Freedom
…Seizing Your Success
…Giving Gratitude
…On the Enlightened Path
…In Spirit
…Finding Life's Passion
…Stories of Transformation
…A Search for Purpose
…Living in Abundance
…Living in Clarity
…The Power of Team
…Wake Up Moments
…Wake Up Moments of Inspiration

Wake Up…Shape Up…Live the Life You Love

Wake Up...
Live the Life You Love
Empowered

TABLE OF CONTENTS

INTRODUCTION

Within this book you will find a wide-ranging assortment of stories concerning personal struggles and triumphs, suggestions and instructions and an entirely new philosophical approach to your life. *Empowered* will help you gain newfound confidence in the area you've been desiring—personal fulfillment.

We live and move in a world of ubiquitous, powerful entities, such as governments and corporations. In these structures of power, many individuals feel cut off and alienated from the wider social unit. They have a hard time fitting in and utilizing their skills to their full potential. In fact, some even doubt their own abilities; they often reach a point when they feel completely powerless.

How is it that we can come to feel this way when we are all highly talented and full of wonderful aspirations and dreams? How did others, who experienced that same lack of belief in themselves finally overcome those feelings and succeed? What example was it that set them free? In *Empowered*, you will find that in many cases, it was the negative self-image they had that was holding them back.

Oftentimes, we feel that we have been allotted a certain status and certain ability by nature, by fate or by family. We are trapped by a certain atmosphere that we feel can never be altered for the better. The answer to this dilemma is *Empowerment*. When we are no longer bound by our environment, we are able to see through this illusion and break free from our determining circumstances. The secret to empowerment is no longer a secret—all you must do is turn the page.

WAKE UP...
LIVE THE LIFE YOU LOVE

Empowered

EMPOWERED—CHOOSING HAPPINESS
Steven E

I lived many years suffering until one day I woke up and found I could make the choice. We can choose to either suffer or be happy.

The only reason you suffer is because you choose to do so whether consciously or unconsciously. Concentrate on all the good you have in your life now, and remember, there are many who are much worse off than you.

Wake up and stop suffering! Stop being the victim. Suffering makes you feel safe because you know it so well. The change can be scary, but also very rewarding!

Pessimistic people are fearful. They are afraid to have faith and hope because of their past. Past failures promote pessimism rather than optimism.

There will always be challenges in life. Prepare yourself, because the more success you achieve, the greater the challenges you face.

Depression, anger or any negative emotion only reflects a state of mind. That state of mind can be changed instantly. Go within and learn why you feel that way. Pull out the root of the negativity from the very bottom of your inner self. If you choose to be happy, not only will you make yourself happy, but you will make those around you happy as well.

The word *inspiration* means to be *infused with spirit*.

Practice what you love each and every day. If you are going to do something, then do it without complaining. Be enthusiastic about your work, your play and your free time. The word "enthusiasm" comes from the Greek root *entheus,* which means to be *filled with God.*

Discard bad habits—pessimism, negativity, judgment, complaining and gossip. Replace them with positives—acceptance, love and kindness—directed at both yourself and others.

Remember: The energy you put out into the world is the energy that will come back to you. Each time you catch yourself becoming cynical and negative, turn your thoughts around 180 degrees. Give yourself quiet time each day to erase feelings of unworthiness. This time of meditation and prayer will nourish your soul and remove any doubts you may have about yourself.

Inspire yourself! Inspire others!

Steven E

BREAK THROUGH
Connie Uthoff

"The first law of success is concentration—to bend all the energies to one point, and to go directly to that point, looking neither to the right, nor to the left."
—William Matthews, Journalist

I am a martial artist. I have black belts in Tang Soo Do and Tae Kwon Do, as well as significant training in Ju Jitsu, Israeli combat techniques and weapons. I have competed both nationally and internationally. While most of my training has involved the external use of technique, power, leverage and redirection of an opponent's energy, one day I was "woken up" by what I considered an unlikely source. I learned a valuable lesson about internal strength, courage, resolve and unwavering commitment to personal success.

It was a Saturday afternoon and our martial arts school was having a belt test. I came to support the students who were testing and to help the master instructor if needed. Most of the day went by as expected and the test drew to a close. Only one portion of the test remained: the board breaking requirement. Two gray cinder blocks sat 18 inches apart on the floor in the center of the room. They were bridged by a one-inch thick pine board. A 9-year-old boy dressed in a traditional do balk (martial arts uniform) stood poised before the structure, preparing for his first break.

The studio fell silent.

Seventy-five students, family members and instructors were watching from seats around the room, waiting for David to complete this final requirement. He paused. To break a board requires focus and concentration, but also proper technique. The concept is to break *through* the board—not to stop at the surface, but to drive all the way through as though you are actually aiming at an imaginary spot beyond the piece of wood.

Finally ready, David lined up his fist on the board, went through two slow motion hammer-fists in preparation: One, two...he took a deep breath and slammed his fist into the board. Nothing happened. Again, one, two, slam...nothing. The room was still. Some people shifted a bit. It can be uncomfortable to witness a failed break, especially on a test. However, David did not lose his resolve. He struck the board at least five more times with no success. Uncomfortable became awkward. Other students were waiting. The air was thick with unease, another failed attempt. Finally, the head instructor came over from his position in front of the room. "Next time," is all he said in a soft voice. What I heard was, "Try again next time," but, to this day, I wonder what David heard. Maybe he thought "next time" meant on his next try because one last time David squared up his stance, focused and with one motion, broke the board and the growing tension in the room.

Over the months and years, David faced larger challenges, competitions and multiple board breaks. As he overcame each new challenge, his confidence and expertise grew. Today he is an instructor with his own school and his students are breaking boards. David's determination produced results. That, in turn, gave him deeper confidence and courage to succeed. He broke through to a life he loves.

That Saturday afternoon, I came into the studio to help, but left with a whole new perspective of strength and power. David overcame some pretty big obstacles for a nine-year-old. In less than 10 minutes, he conquered fear, uncertainty and doubt until his internal focus matched his physical ability to apply the technique properly, breaking through to new potential and opportunity. He could have quit, but he didn't. Instead, he gained even greater confidence and taught the power of perseverance to those watching. Many people, myself included, would not have risked the embarrassment of failing eight times publicly in order to succeed. I have since learned that failure is often a part of success. Remember that Edison failed count-less times, but it is his achievement that we will always remember and appreciate.

To possess such determination is to have an added tool for creating a life of possibility. It takes incredible courage and dedication to go after the life you desire. Who knows what would have happened if David gave up? Would he have the life he loves today? What do you need to do to break through?

Since then, I have noticed that the breakthrough principles that helped David are the same principles that drive success in other areas of life, including health and fitness, business, relationships, sports and education. I like to call these "break through principles to life success." They include, but are not limited to, setting goals, envision-ing the end result, utilizing proper technique, planning, committing to your own success, persevering, focusing and breaking through.

As you develop and face new experiences that come into your life, your original goals may change. You may develop techniques and skills that lead you in an entirely new direction and you may wake up to even greater possibilities than you could ever imagine. Stop, refocus and move forward, always staying committed to your life of possibility. Like David's case, as we wake up to ourselves, our dreams and our passions, we will have obstacles. We will have our own "boards" to break through, our own challenges to overcome. Some may come in the form of poor timing or financial constraints; some may be momentary blocks. Others may take eight or nine strikes to overcome. As you continue your journey, remember to look past and through your challenges to the other side. They are a part of growth, part of your life test. So, like David, don't give up. Square up, focus and break through to the life you have always wanted to live.

Connie Uthoff

AWAKENING THE GIANT WITHIN!
Dr. Anand Menon

Like every other person ever created in the history of mankind, I was born to achieve, to excel and to be a blessing to humanity in my own special way. I was destined to be uniquely beautiful and capable like no other. All of us were born this way–born to demonstrate magnificent, inherent power and to become a source of inspiration to every person with whom we come in contact.

Like every other person on this planet, I was born to do exactly that! And, like most people, I lost that belief in myself. Somewhere along the way, I allowed people, circumstances and untruths to enter my life. I chose to accept mediocre beliefs and build mediocre value systems that would govern my life for nearly 30 years. I allowed the powerful giant in me to remain in a slumber and awoke a dwarf instead. This dwarf manifested itself in every aspect of my life because I permitted it to do so. This was reflected in my lifestyle, my relationships, my jobs and my outlook on life. The single most damaging influence of my personal dwarf was the fact that I allowed myself to think of my circumstances as being beyond my control. I chose to tell myself I was given the "flip side" of the deal.

I found easy solutions to all my problems. I even had a secret weapon that I called the "setback getback." For every setback in my life, I "got back" at the people and the circumstances responsible. My family was extremely dysfunctional. I watched my father cut himself open and try to commit suicide. My teachers just never understood me. Life was always going to be unfair. I would never be good looking. I didn't have the college degrees others had. God was too busy to glance in my direction. The list was endless and I was in a downward spiral. You name the setback, I had the "getback!" I allowed myself to

get into trouble with people, with work and with the authorities. I allowed the dwarf inside me to become a giant—one that was never meant to be there.

Deep within, I knew I had been created for a purpose. I knew I was meant to be bigger than everything in my life at the time. I never knew it by name, but I understood the influence and impact of the Law of Attraction. I had given it my own name. I called it the "Law of Association." As I spent hours contemplating my life, I realized I was slowly morphing and becoming the dwarf that was inside me. I knew that my feelings and actions were the result of focusing energy on the negative outcomes. My Law of Association made me realize one simple, but earth-shaking and life-changing truth: We become that with which we associate ourselves!

It was 1996 when my first wake-up moment happened. I began to seek answers where, in the past, I had only questions. I reached for the sacred scriptures. I searched for the One who is bigger than me and who would help me discover my own purpose in life. I found God while I was at home by myself reading His Scriptures. I expected it to be a spectacular moment, but it happened very quietly and very silently one afternoon. Nobody but me knew it had even happened, but that was what mattered the most! Almost instantly, the sleeping giant within me stirred. When I look back over the past 10 years of my life, I am always amazed at what I achieved when I changed my thinking.

I replaced the "setback getback" way of thinking with a "payback getback" thought process. As my life was transformed, miracles began to happen daily. I began to believe in myself and my potential. I felt good about myself and my life. I placed God in the midst of all my circumstances. The outcome brought me to my knees in gratitude every single time. The miracles happened in all areas of my life, including the physical, financial, personal, spiritual and relationship aspects.

In 2000, I was diagnosed with macular degeneration of the right eye (progressive blindness), but God changed that by healing me at a spiritual retreat. I believed and acted out my faith. I thought, felt and behaved as if I were whole and, as a result, I became whole. Eight years later, both my eyes are intact and I can see perfectly.

I had always felt insecure about my inadequacy regarding education and my qualifications. When I began to believe I was qualified, I felt and acted like I was. I focused my positive energy on knowledge acquisition and obtaining my degree. I acquired my master's degree in business administration and went on to achieve a doctoral degree in psychology. Over the past 10 years, I have acquired 15 international certifications and accreditations in human behavior profiling systems. I am currently working toward a master's degree in theology with plans for a double doctorate in Bible studies.

On the professional front, my career skyrocketed. I have now consulted, trained and coached several thousand people in the UK, the Asian sub-continent, the Middle East and Africa. My professional training and life transformational exposure workshops and modules have been delivered to audiences ranging from 10 to more than 50,000 people.

I have worked in senior management positions in the Middle East with dynamic business conglomerates like Emirates Airline, DAMAC Holding and Le Meridien Hotels. I have also worked closely with

CEOs, internationally acclaimed speakers and entrepreneurs to deliver training and learning values in 12 countries.

I am currently the vice president of training and development for a business conglomerate overseeing the needs of 10 diverse businesses in 18 countries. My current role has contributed to the corporation's growth from an annual turnover of $1 billion to more than $2 billion in my second year, with a jump to $6 billion in the third year. I am also currently working on establishing my own Bible study ministry called "Life in the Word Ministries."

My vision is to change the world one soul at a time. In the past decade, I have produced more than 440 audio CD recordings of spiritual teachings that have helped thousands of teenagers, young adults, couples and families discover their spiritual potential and get in touch with their faith.

If you are reading this, then let me say this with certainty: The time to take control of your life has come. Somewhere inside you, you have discovered you were meant to be much more, that your life was meant to be lived in abundance, and that you are worth much more than you currently see. The opportunity has presented itself to you today. Put your signature on this planet. Leave your mark. The moment has arrived. How will you seize it? What will you do with it? I look forward to meeting you where it matters and where you should be, at the top!

Dr. Anand Menon

CREATING MY LIFE
Margit L. Cruice

A friend of mine passed away this week at the age of 50. It was an ordinary heart attack, but completely unexpected. It was a reminder to me of how short life can be and how suddenly it can be taken away. For many people, a tragedy like this is the reason they "wake up" and begin to live. But, if we don't have a tragedy, what does it take to create the life we love?

I learned years ago that we create our own lives. Only recently did I realize we are responsible for creating *everything* in our lives. For instance, things weren't working out in my marriage, and it was easier to blame my husband than to look at how I might be contributing to the problem. Another time, when my business wasn't going according to plan, it was because I didn't have the proper time to invest in it. I was focused on everything except for the reality that I was creating these problems.

As I blamed external forces for where I was in my life, I was disempowered. There wasn't much I could do about what was happening and my change came about as I studied my way through a life coaching course. I knew without a doubt that life coaching was for me, but I didn't know how much work I had to do first regarding my own mentality. Over two and a half years, I learned that by taking responsibility for what I created and what I was creating in my life, I would be empowered to make changes. I had the power to create anything I wanted!

I knew that if I could create anything, I didn't need to place limits on myself. Somewhere along life's journey my dreams became smaller instead of bigger. During my "marketing years," I was told to make sure my goals were achievable and realistic, which led me to scale down what I thought I could achieve. I've had to step out of that idea and now my dreams involve global speaking opportunities and the ability to help thousands of people—not just those I can coach one-on-one. I'm not there yet, but these dreams give me motivation and drive and, more importantly, I believe I can achieve them.

Even when I finished my coaching course, external factors played a part in where my business was headed. My husband was diagnosed with cancer just after I graduated. We had another business partnership, but I didn't normally work in it. As my husband went through chemotherapy I had to take on a lot of the work in the business, so I put my coaching aside. We also had three active young children and a house to maintain. What got me through those months were the perspectives I had learned through coaching. Every moment provided me with a learning opportunity and the chance to see how strong I was on the inside.

It was during this period that I realized it was time for me to move away from my marriage. This was one of my all-time biggest fears for the sake of myself, my children and my husband. Telling him our marriage was over was one of the hardest things I have ever done, but it gave me a sense of overwhelming relief and freedom. I was now on the path to creating the life I truly wanted.

In those few months, life continued to throw things at us. Our business was going badly and would be difficult to sell. The block of land we needed to sell sat unsold for months. Even as I went through this, I knew I was helping to create these situations. I was even grateful for the experiences because I was learning so much about what I truly wanted, about how I created things in my life and about how I dealt with them.

My coaching business began to thrive. I was offered paid speaking opportunities to talk about what I truly love: fearless living. I could stand in the knowledge that I was living fearlessly regardless of what was happening in my life. I knew I was in the process of creating an extraordinary future, and that knowledge came with a sense of peace and clarity.

All the while, I kept reminding myself I was creating my future, but it was equally important to enjoy where I was at the time. There was no point living with the thought that "things will be better when...." I had to enjoy every moment because I would never get them back. Throughout my husband's treatments, our business failure and our impending divorce, I was able to have fun because I focused on helping other people. There is nothing like putting your own problems aside for awhile and making a difference in someone else's life!

Coming through these traumas, I am now in a very peaceful place. I am extraordinarily happy and I know I can handle whatever is thrown my way. As I work through a divorce, I do so with a loving heart and wish my ex-husband only good things. My business is steadily growing; clients come to me now, as do speaking opportunities. I am making a difference in my children's school as the P&C President, and I am having so much fun!

I have huge dreams that I am working toward, but I enjoy each day. I know without a doubt that I create my life and I am changing my reality day by day. I know opportunities are coming my way, and I just need to see them and take the ones that make sense to me. I know I will not fail at anything I try because everything is a learning opportunity. This week I know the fragility of life and how quickly it can be taken away. This, too, will become an inspiration to me—an impetus to create the life I truly love.

Margit L. Cruice

JUST SWING AND LET GO
Nicole Brandon

I spent one Saturday afternoon taking a trapeze class. I am not suggesting that you rush out and take a trapeze class; it's just how I like to spend a peaceful afternoon. During my first class, I was 25 feet in the air when the catcher said the most important thing anyone has ever said to me: "Don't look for me. Don't reach for me. I'm the catcher, I will catch you. It is your job simply to swing and let go."

I have since lived my life like this. From that moment on, I swing and let go. I trust I am going to be caught in life and I fly with such height, speed, freedom and velocity that my imagination twirls with delight, euphoric bliss and exhilaration from one moment to the next.

Some say I am a contortionist. Test me to see if it's true. I am able to be flexible and bend with the will of nature and take my body to places of exploration and wonder.

I have a story, a secret, a miracle, an epiphany and a door.

In 2001, I was hit by a drunk driver. My car exploded with a sonic boom and a thrust of light in the air. I watched in awe as the flames floated from above the horrifying wreckage. Peering in from the universe, I was amazed at my death. My body was gone, I had disintegrated. The blaze danced furiously for spectators, with burning heat still raging and colors luminating in an effervescent glow.

"Should I call the police?"

"What?"

"Ma'am? Should I call the police?"

"You can see me?"

I was alive!

The doctors said my career was over. No movement, no flight, no sauntering the earth, no sitting, no thrill, no dancing, no adventure, no life, no more.

How is that possible?

I remember lying in the hospital and crying harder than I had ever cried before. Then I heard a voice, a memory, a statement to change my life, to change my world, exactly like "just swing and let go." This time, I heard my mother. I was four years old and I had spilled some milk. "Honey, why are you crying?" She was cradling me.

Peacefully, she said, "Why are you crying? It's just an accident. Why are you crying? It's just an accident, we just need to clean up the mess."

Yes! It was just an accident, and I just needed to clean up the mess and everything would be fine.

A year later I climbed the Great Wall of China. A year after I was told my physical life was over, I danced around the world and leapt through the sky. Today, I teach physical transformation and physical regeneration, but it was the "words;" it was the message, the power of a thought. The second in time that I shifted like a kaleidoscope, I saw a new view of beauty, glory, magic and perfection. What words have been spoken that move you to stardom, to success, to paradise, to freedom, to happiness, to glory, to the brilliance of your life and the beauty and the power of you? Was it a kind word, a positive thought, an act of encouragement, a guiding hand? What gave you a new perspective, a broader view, allowing you to release fear, trust instincts and reach for your dreams? What words let you swing, fly, let go and bathe in the delight and freedom of your life and its infinite possibilities? What words etch, define and inspire you?

Reach, dream, fly, or, you can always on a sultry afternoon, take a trapeze class and hear what the catcher has to say.

Nicole Brandon

NEW BEGINNINGS
Jana Pounder

It was a lovely room with dark hardwood floors and golden walls, a huge, rock fireplace in the corner and wooden shutters on the windows. A big screen TV played the tennis match Bea had been looking forward to watching, but her mind kept drifting. She felt unnaturally lonely and depressed. She and her husband had just moved their family from Idaho to Arizona, and she wished with all her heart that it were possible to turn back time. She had loved her life. It had been routine and comfortable with many good friendships.

She wished her friends were beside her now, talking over each other, rehashing troubles, remembering old gossip and funny stories. They'd known she hated to feel gloomy. It felt heavy, like wearing every article of clothing in your closet at once. Bea always handled her difficulties in the same way—by putting on her old Cubs hat and spending time in her yard, touching the petals of flowers, watering and feeding them, planting new ones. She'd have done that now if they hadn't moved to Phoenix, and it wasn't the middle of July, and it wasn't over 110 degrees in the shade! Who wants to live in a place where eggs could fry on the sidewalk?

Her husband, Sam, had taken a new position with his company as manager of a manufacturing unit, something he'd wanted and worked toward for over a year. Now that they had moved and he was putting in 10-hour days and her daughter was enrolled in her new school, Bea felt lost and alone.

She loved her husband and wanted to be happy, but his joy wasn't her joy. She'd had a life she really loved. She had recently been pro-

moted to marketing manager within the company where she had
worked; her three best friends worked there, too. There were always
lots of opinions, lots of laugher, lots of differences, lots of comfort. "I
miss my old life," she muttered at the TV.

Keri, her 14-year-old daughter, came dancing down the stairs and
began rummaging through the many boxes they had stacked in the
family room, looking for a book she just *had* to read. Keri was a tall,
thin, pretty girl with braces, big feet and curly blonde hair.

"Keri," Bea asked. "What did you label your boxes when you packed
them?"

Keri raised her head and looked at her mom with the pained look
she sometimes gets when she wants to say, "Duh!" but knows her
mom would object.

"I put 'MINE' on them, but it must have rubbed off 'cause it's not
on any of the boxes here. Maybe they didn't pack mine in the truck!
Maybe they're still in Idaho with the rest of my life!" she wailed.

Bea had heard different words but the same tone coming from Keri
since they'd made the decision to move. She wished she could tell
Keri that she understood, but the thought that her mom could
understand how she felt had ended with Keri's 14th birthday. She'd
grown up. Although she loved her mom, Bea had become "old."

Bea didn't want to tell her that last night their old neighbors had
called and asked what they were planning to do with the six boxes
left on the side of the driveway. Yes, Keri's boxes were probably there.
The van lines would be delivering the boxes in two days. Needing a
distraction, Bea suggested they drive to a bookstore, browse the new

release aisle and maybe pick up a new book or two. Keri turned toward her mom, a combination of suspicion and derision in her eyes. "Do you know where one is and how to get there?"

At that moment, Bea's cell phone buzzed. The sudden joy of seeing it was her best friend, Jill, was followed by a twinge of worry for Jill's four-year-old daughter, Ziggy. It had been a little over a year since Ziggy had been diagnosed with leukemia and had gone through all the treatments. Everyone thought she was coming along great until a month ago when the doctors found the cancer had returned. Ziggy had hated the restrictions and sickness that came with the process of fighting the disease, and Jill didn't know how to tell her that she had to go through it again.

Jill was calling to say Ziggy had died that morning. She shared with Bea their last evening together. "My sweet Ziggy hadn't been doing so well yesterday afternoon, and by the end of the day, she was almost completely unresponsive and limp. Around midnight, I carried her from the sofa to the bedroom and put her in bed."

Jill said her six-year-old daughter, Carol, had awakened and come into the room, climbed onto her lap, and that together they had held onto Ziggy's hands. They spoke of some of their greatest moments together. They had laughed and cried together. Jill told Ziggy that she had served a great purpose and touched more lives than she knew. She promised that all of this would not be in vain and that they would make sure they made their lives count. Most importantly, she let her know how much they loved her and that if she wanted to let go, it was okay and she would be at peace.

Then, Jill and Carol crawled in bed with her, one on each side. Jill said she lay awake and around three that morning, when she put her hand on Ziggy's chest, she felt her struggle to breathe and noticed her heart was not beating as it should.

Jill said she had prayed that Ziggy would not suffer and, 15 minutes later, felt her stop breathing. She said that in that instant, Ziggy's entire face relaxed and she had the most beautiful look of peace. Jill said she knew God had answered her prayers.

It was the hardest thing Bea had ever listened to, but she offered the help and friendship she knew Jill needed. Jill's words were words of gratitude and strength for the new journey God had prepared for her.

Bea woke in her new home the next morning as a new person. She thanked God for the beautiful sunshine, for the new flowers that she could tend, for the people in her life that she loved, for the blessings of new beginnings. She'd seen how change was handled in the most difficult of times and realized she could do nothing but give it her best and live every minute of it.

She heard Keri at the door. "Mom, the moving van is here and they are unloading more boxes." She waited for the earth shattering wail. "They did leave my boxes in Idaho! I told you so!"

Jana Pounder

WHAT QUESTION FOCUSES YOUR LIFE?
Dr. David Yeh

How many times have you heard, "Questions control the conversation; questions control your thoughts; questions empower your life?" Do you find it difficult to apply these aphorisms and theories to real life? I did until a question woke me up and pointed me toward a life that I love.

What do you do for a living? Depending upon the time of day and context my answers to that question range from "I'm a radiologist and nuclear physician and I help doctors like yours figure out what's wrong with you" to "I study and teach Tai Chi" to "I trade the equities markets." How do these areas relate to each other? Quite simply, I asked myself a single question long ago, "What is the secret of life?"

That question came to mind when I encountered an opportunity in college to study anything I wanted, as long as I could show that I strongly desired to study a subject that did not fit neatly into any certain major. Sure, it was an ambitious endeavor, but why not tackle it? Isn't this one of the big questions people have asked for ages? I only knew one thing: Even if I couldn't find an easy answer, the journey would certainly be interesting. I immediately applied and was accepted into the program.

The Secret of Life
Part of the beauty of the question was the complexity—no single viewpoint held any uniquely tangible answer. My journey started with sciences—biology led me to microbiology and, in turn, to molecular and cellular biology, which led to quantum mechanics and the philosophy of the ultimate order of the universe itself. As I stud-

ied smaller and smaller systems, the problems of bigger systems—from integrated biospheres to interdependent solar systems and celestial mechanics—seemed to play inseparable roles in the scientific understanding of life. The question, "What defines 'life?'" became an increasingly important one to answer. For, without boundaries to define life, I might as well have studied the question, "What is the nature of the universe?" Perhaps it was the very definition of life that was its secret, yet the more I studied, the more the boundaries blurred.

Is Life an Illusion?
People from every culture seem to have their own particular opinions on life. What is interesting isn't the various opinions of life itself, but the thought processes that have derived from those opinions. Just the rich range of philosophies that have survived to this day reflects how inseparable psychology is from the development of cultures and the paradigms through which we filter our ideas on existence.

As college ended, I pondered my next step in life. One logical path resulting from the search for the secret of life led me to the question, "What is the secret of human life?" This naturally led me to medical school. Despite numerous options, I chose and focused upon that one question for the time.

What Medical Specialty Should I Pursue?
Most medical students either fall in love with a specialty immediately, or think long and hard to decide. I was one of the lucky students who enjoyed each field I encountered. Choosing a specialty was a difficult decision until I realized that everyone in almost every field I rotated through had to consult a radiologist at some time or another. A radiologist is the doctor's doctor. Because almost every type of

physician will consult them, radiologists must know something about every area of medicine and integrate that knowledge with information about the technology they use. I could see that I would be able to impact the lives of patients directly every day. The more I practiced, the more I honed my knowledge of the field. Truly, rocket science meets neurosurgery in the quest of understanding life at a practical level.

Is Science the Only Way to Look at Life?
In diagnostic imaging, science is the only paradigm we've got. However, I also experienced firsthand the healing effects of Tai Chi during medical school. I can think of no other art form that manifests itself as a physical philosophy. Tai Chi can be described as a martial art, a tool for healing, an exercise, a meditation or a tool for dealing with stress. Tai Chi is a method of examining and experiencing life through a completely different paradigm, complete with practical applications to inner and outer health, as well as to our relationship to the universe. In practice, there is immediate feedback to our understanding of life, as well as side effects of long-term health.

What is the secret of life? In my 20 years of studying that very question, I have found paths that give me great joy every day. The quality of your life will be reflected by the quality of the questions you ask yourself. Empower yourself. Ask good questions. And most importantly, find the questions that focus your life.

Dr. David Yeh

EMBRACE SILENCE
Dr. Wayne W. Dyer®

You live in a noisy world, constantly bombarded with loud music, sirens, construction equipment, jet airplanes, rumbling trucks, leaf blowers, lawn mowers and tree cutters. These manmade, unnatural sounds invade your senses and keep silence at bay.

In fact, you've been raised in a culture that not only eschews silence, but is terrified of it. The car radio must always be on, and any pause in conversation is a moment of embarrassment that most people quickly fill with chatter. For many, being alone in silence is pure torture.

The famous scientist Blaise Pascal observed, "All man's miseries derive from not being able to sit quietly in a room alone."

With practice, you can become aware that there's a momentary silence in the space between your thoughts. In this silent space, you'll find the peace that you crave in your daily life. You'll never know that peace if you don't have any spaces between your thoughts.

The average person is said to have 60,000 separate thoughts a day. With so many thoughts, there are almost no gaps. If you could reduce that number by half, you would open up an entire world of possibilities for yourself. For it is when you merge into the silence, and become one with it, that you reconnect to your source and know the peacefulness that some call "God." It is stated beautifully in Psalms of the Old Testament: "Be still and know that I am God." The key words are "still" and "know."

"Still" actually means "silence." Mother Teresa described silence and its relationship to God by saying, "God is the friend of silence. See how nature (trees, grass) grows in silence. We need silence to be able to touch souls." This includes your soul.

It's really the space between the notes that make the music you enjoy so much. Without the spaces, all you would have is one continuous, noisy note. Everything that's created comes out of silence. Your thoughts emerge from the nothingness of silence. Your words come out of this void. Your very essence emerged from emptiness.

All creativity requires some stillness. Your sense of inner peace depends on spending some of your life energy in silence to recharge your batteries, removing tension and anxiety, thus reacquainting you with the joy of knowing God and feeling closer to all of humanity. Silence reduces fatigue and allows you to experience your own creative juices.

The second word in the Old Testament observation, "know," refers to making your personal and conscious contact with God. To know God is to banish doubt and become independent of others' definitions and descriptions of God. Instead, you have your own personal knowing. And, as Melville reminded us so poignantly, "God's one and only voice is silence."

Dr. Wayne W. Dyer®

TWO BOOMERS IN THE (K)NOW
Shelley Berger Dooley, P.M.H.N.P. & Melanie R. Schockett, Ph.D.

We are the first generation to arrive at midlife since the women's movement of the 1970s, and thus we find ourselves in uncharted territory for which there are no guidelines. We are leaving behind early adulthood and embarking upon the remaining chapters in our lives, aware that time is limited. Yet, we have few role models from the earlier generations and our generation has never quite followed the rules!

Unlike our parents, we choose not to be held hostage by the judgments of others. As we strive to shed the constraints of the self-consciousness that we carried for years, we feel more energized, empowered and in touch with our passions and vitality. Our actions are more fully experienced in the NOW as we aspire to live each day to the fullest and to recreate ourselves. The possibilities seem endless and we are free to take risks which previous generations would never dared to have considered.

The challenges of midlife are many, including the departure of children from the home, the care of ailing parents, the loss of loved ones and the loss of abilities once possessed. The following passages exemplify how we have traversed some of these challenges and emerged more empowered by living in the NOW.

Shelley Berger Dooley

One of my earliest memories was of my father comforting me. I was crying because I was terribly anxious about my own death. How does a girl of 10 develop such fear?

One possibility may be another memory—a memory of my mother pacing and worrying about my father when he was late coming home from work. Invariably, he had missed the train or the train had simply been delayed. He was perfectly fine, but Mom had worried. She worried a lot.

She was a loving and devoted mother, but anxiety pervaded her personality at times. She worried about the norms of society and about the repercussions that would follow if we strayed. Fear for our safety laced her instructions and warnings to us. She imagined scenarios that would never have entered my mind. It is no wonder that, years later, I embodied her anxieties about health, safety, the future and what others thought of me. All of this worry eventually manifested into panic attacks and bothersome heart palpitations in early adulthood.

Decades later, my mom developed Alzheimer's disease. I watched as she became more anxious and experienced panic attacks. She was overwhelmed by simple tasks because her brain could no longer process normally.

Eventually, she went to Phoenix and lived for a number of years at an assisted living facility there. As awful as the disease was, it actually relieved her of anxiety for a period of time. All she could do was experience the present. Surprisingly, she became funny, happy, relaxed and totally in the NOW. She did not choose this state of mind; the disease decided it for her. Mom would burst into song at random; a word would trigger a song or a rhyme. She was funny, positive and content. She now revealed a side of herself I had not seen before because it had been hidden beneath anxiety and fear.

Seeing her living joyfully in the present was a powerful lesson to me about letting go of fears. I saw what happened to someone when they remained exclusively in the present, and it was wonderful. She became my guru—my spiritual teacher. The woman who had modeled anxiety for me now showed me the way out; the value of NOW was in my face and I finally recognized it.

My brain can and does occasionally travel to the past where regrets and self-criticisms lurk. Likewise, it can and does travel to the future where it imagines awful scenarios as my mom did when I was a child. However, my trips to the land of fears are much less frequent and, when they emerge, I am able to tap into the childlike wonder of my mom singing or spouting spontaneous rhymes. Then I smile, breathe and reconnect to my present space. She taught me from the depths of her disease the beauty and wonder of being in the present and valuing the NOW. Now I kNOW.

Melanie R. Schockett

I disconnected my 68-year-old mother from the ventilator on my wedding anniversary. Her death was unexpected since she had entered the hospital only days before. Although she was unable to speak, when she was fully disconnected, she opened her eyes and looked directly at me as if to say, "Goodbye." What emerged from my being was even more unexpected: a primordial wail, the likes of which I had never heard.

Of course, I had no idea at that time that my husband, at 42 years of age, would suffer a similar fate only two months later. I can still recall my daughter saying, "Mommy, what are those funny noises Daddy is making?" He died in our living room as I frantically waited for the ambulance to arrive. The hardest phone call I had to make was to my mother-in-law to tell her that her second son had died. The most heart-wrenching disclosures were to my children: my third-grade daughter and my kindergartener son.

The two people I had known most intimately in my 40 years had vanished; I was lost. After the loss of my mother, my father fell apart; he became psychotic and was dependent on me within a year of her death. My forties were not kind as other losses of friends and the illnesses of my children followed closely on one another. However, something miraculous happened when I reached 50. Hope was restored and I was joyous at having reached that landmark. I began a rebirthing process.

Soon after turning 50, I walked up to the trainer's desk at a local gym and, with tears in my eyes, I said, "I need help." The treadmill became my addiction as I found that I could run off all my frustrations and angst.

Tentatively, at first, I started dating. I was prompted to do so when I overheard my teenaged daughter predict that she would, eventually, have to take care of me.

I awoke to the beauty all around me: the sunshine, the breezes and the mountains. I started to dance. I had always been extremely self-conscious about dancing—I was a klutz who could not keep the beat. Now, in my fifties, I am able to dance with abandon, with joy, and with passion. Thirteen years after that sad period of personal loss, I feel sensual, alive and youthful. I am excited over the myriad possibilities. I am grateful for every moment.

Sometimes, I wonder who I would be if I had not undergone all the trauma that unfolded, but I enjoy the person I am now. I NOW know that I can weather any storm and I have an inner strength I never imagined possible. If, along the way I start feeling over-whelmed, I focus on being in my body through dance, exercise or meditation. Being in my body inevitably returns me to the present. NOW I kNOW.

* * * *

As Boomers, we continue to change the rules by which we live. We will not go into midlife and beyond focused on the memories of our lives, relaxing in our rocking chairs. Our kNOWledge, gleaned from years of experience, can only be fully realized when in the NOW, for NOW is central to kNOWledge. To be in the kNOW is to be in the NOW.

Shelley Berger Dooley, P.M.H.N.P. & Melanie R. Schockett, Ph.D.

PADDLING LIFE'S RIVER
Dr. Brett Dunningham

When I was 16 years old an event occurred that changed the way I looked at my life as well as life in general.

Although I took them for granted at the time, I look back now at how unique my teen years really were. I was a member of the Boys Brigade (like Boy Scouts), and by the age of 18, I had climbed some of New Zealand's highest mountains, hiked and explored some of the most beautiful and rugged areas of my country and had many other exciting adventures. I was a somewhat rebellious fellow, often not towing the line on how things should be done. Officers of the company took me aside more than once. I guess I had too much of that youthful sort of selfishness.

On one such journey, we were on a 10-day canoeing trip down one of New Zealand's longest rivers, the Wanganui River. The head of the river was steep, with many exciting rapids, and it became quieter later where the river met the ocean. There were about 14 of us on the trip, and we had eight single-man fiberglass canoes and three two-man wooden canvas canoes. We had built the canoes ourselves and trained for a year prior to the trip on how to look after ourselves on the river. I had built my own fiberglass canoe and was proud of my efforts.

We all knew each other well from many prior adventures. The previous year, we got lost in dense bush for six days until we were rescued by an army helicopter. Well, not exactly rescued—we refused to be picked up, so after being shown the way, we walked out, but that's another story entirely.

A good friend of mine on the journey was Michael. I can't remember how he received the nickname, but we all just called him "Wobbly." He was a lovely lad who smiled a lot and had long, brown curly hair. Everyone liked him. He had a wonderful talent for cartoon drawing and if any of us got into an embarrassing situation (which was quite often), we would find a piece of paper secured to our tent the next day depicting the event. He also made sure it was in the next copy of our newsletter.

On the ninth day of our journey the river seemed to calm down. We had just departed from a little settlement known as Bethlehem after lunch. There hadn't been much rain and the river level was lower than usual. We arrived at a right-hand bend in the river. All the water was being diverted down a narrow channel on the left side, so it was running fast. On the right side was a flat area of rocks that normally would have been under water.

On this occasion, I was the second canoe down. As I sped down the channel, I noticed there was a tree that had fallen partially across the river and, as I had gone too far to the left, I was heading straight for it. My canoe broadsided it. The force of the river held me and there seemed to be no way to free myself. I was tempted to tip my canoe over and come up the other side, but at that point I was the only one on the trip who had not yet spilled out into the rapids and I was keen on keeping my record. However, I would soon discover that my ego had saved my life.

As the other canoeists floated by, they could see the problem and managed to stay clear. One of the last canoes down was a two-man wooden canoe paddled by my friends John and Wobbly. I could see they were also traversing down the river too far to the left and they couldn't do anything about it. Their boat smashed into my canoe and the log. The power of the river broke the canoe in two. John went around the front and floated free, but Wobbly went under my canoe, turned upside down and became trapped underneath in a mangle of branches and roots. I could see the wooden base of his canoe about 12 inches under the water below me, but I wasn't sure how to get to it. I also knew we were in a spot no one else could reach. I realized I had to get out of my canoe, so I released my splash cover and climbed onto the log. My friend was only a foot away, but I didn't know how to reach him.

I reached for the camping knife that was sheathed around my waist and tried stabbing into the wooden base of the canoe. We had made the canoes strong, and the knife just seemed to bounce off the frame. Time went by with little results. Suddenly, the knife slipped through my wet hand and sliced my fingers, but it didn't seem important at the time. I remember looking up at my friends who had, by now, pulled up their canoes on the flat area of rocks on the right and saw the look of horror and disbelief on their faces. Soon, 20 minutes had gone by and we realized we weren't going to get Wobbly out of there. A few hours later, a jet boat came up the river, and with a chainsaw, freed the boat and our friend. The trip was over.

Many of us lose friends when we are young, but this had a profound effect on me. I was so near and yet so far. It made me realize how precious life is and how, at any moment, we can lose it. I spent two more years with the Boys Brigade and received many awards and certificates, eventually leaving as an NCO to start my chiropractic training in the United States.

That event changed my view on life and, as a healer, I have always tried to encourage patients to live their lives better and more abundantly. Our lives can change any time; this event changed mine. I agree with what John Lennon once said: "Life is what happens to you when you're busy making other plans."

Dr. Brett Dunningham

DEFINING SUCCESS
Michelle R. McConville

What does success mean to me? Success means wealth, position, honor. Success means living in the right house in the right location. Success means being married to the right spouse, sending your children to the right school. Success means a successful performance or achievement. Success means achieving fame or triumphing over another. Success is a state of mind.

How does one determine that success has been achieved? Is it possible to achieve success and be satisfied with what we have? If we set a goal and achieve it, do we celebrate and feel satisfied with our accomplishment?

People may have had the impression that I was successful. I was married, had two wonderful children who would make any parent proud, I owned my own home and had two cars in the garage. I had loving parents and good friends. Professionally, I had a good position with a good salary and worked for a good company. I was given opportunities to travel to faraway places. In reality, I was over it—overweight, overworked, overtired, overstressed and in complete denial.

Reality hit me upside the head when I burned out. My body and mind crashed so badly I could barely function. Then I began the exhausting cycle of doctor appointments and tests. The test results showed serious health issues. It was time to face reality and make some major life-changing decisions.

My first decision was to research options to improve my health.

Taking prescribed medications was not an option for me. I feel that medications just mask symptoms and often cause side effects that are as bad as or worse than the condition they are meant to relieve. I had to own up to what I had done to myself and take the responsibility of fixing it. The first step was to research the various programs that were reported to help with weight loss, including a procedure to reduce the size of my stomach. While it did appear that these programs would help with weight loss, it didn't seem that that they would help me to resolve my health issues.

A friend shared with me a nutrition program I had never heard of. After thoroughly researching the program and its products, looking for excuses to say that it wouldn't work for me, I decided to try it out for 30 days to see what would happen. To date, I have met my weight management goals and my doctors are amazed with the results. I am very satisfied with the results and celebrate each success I reach.

My second decision was to end my unhappy marriage.

It's easy to place all the blame on your spouse. I would lie to myself by saying, "We would be happy if only he would end his addictions; we would be happy if only he would be financially responsible; we would be happy if only he would stop being so negative; we would be happy if only he loved me like I deserve to be loved; we would be happy if only he would talk to me rather than yell." If only he…. I had been playing the victim of my circumstances. However, I had actively participated in those circumstances. Rather than wishing he would change, I began the process of making changes in myself.

I knew that I would not be ready to divorce until I could walk away without anger, bitterness or blame. To accomplish this, I had some forgiving to do. I had to not only forgive him, but myself as well. I had to forgive myself for being unhealthy and overweight. I had to forgive myself for not balancing my home and work life. I had to forgive myself for not standing up and demanding that I be treated the way I knew I should be. During the forgiveness process, an incredible peace and calm came over me. This progressed into a feeling of great inner strength.

By letting go of the negative emotions, I stood straighter, held my head higher and put a smile on my face. I felt free and my heart was happy. I was able to think with clarity and focus. It was time to begin the divorce process. Thankfully, we were able to work together to an amicable end. I am satisfied with the success of the two of us being single and forging a new relationship—one of friendship.

My third decision was to leave corporate America.

My work load and long hours had contributed to some of the issues with my health as well as my issues at home. I have to admit this was the hardest and scariest decision of the three. I loved the people and the work that kept me challenged. I had a good reputation and had won awards. There were many career opportunities, including education, networking and travel. I felt that what I did was a big part of who I was. Without this job, would I lose my identity? Would I cease to exist to my friends at work? Would my family think I was crazy to leave my job, considering that I was newly single and would have no income, no benefits?

I am now an independent business owner for the same nutrition program that has made a positive impact in many areas of my life. I work to inspire others to view themselves as the person they can become. I am more than satisfied with the success of this decision as I share with others the path to a balanced life of health, financial freedom and time with their families.

The decisions I made have allowed me to take back control of my life. These past months have not been easy, nor do I wish they had been. As each challenge was overcome, the wisdom and skills gained helped me to become a better person. Each day I wake up loving life and looking forward to new opportunities.

This chapter started with the questions, "What does success mean?" and "How does one determine that success has been achieved?"

In my opinion, the answer to both questions may be found in the following quote: "To laugh often and much; to win the respect of intelligent people and the affection of children; to earn the appreciation of honest critics and endure the betrayal of false friends; to appreciate beauty; to find the best in others; to leave the world a little better, whether by a healthy child, a garden patch or a redeemed social condition; to know even one life has breathed easier because you have lived. This is to have succeeded."—Ralph Waldo Emerson.

My wish for each reader is that you will find a way to serve others so you may find your personal greatness and success.

Michelle R. McConville

SEE WHAT YOU WANT
Bill Harris

Until about age 40, I was definitely not living the life I loved. I was chronically angry, often depressed, and had one abysmal relationship after another. I had no real career and no idea how to create one. The direction of my life was down or, at best, sideways.

This was all a blessing in disguise though, because it created an intense motivation to learn what happy, peaceful and successful people did that I wasn't doing.

Today, I'm married to a wonderful woman who really loves me. I make 10 times what I used to fantasize about. Plus, I have a challenging career doing something I love.

My anger problem is gone, and I haven't been depressed for even a minute in nearly 15 years.

Now, at age 54, I truly am living the life I love. This transformation happened when I discovered a few key principles that created tremendous positive change for me. They will work for you, too.

What are these secrets?

First, happy people acknowledge that they are creating their reality internally and externally. They see circumstances as influential, but know that what they do inside creates how they feel and behave and which people and situations they draw to themselves.

For most people, processing external circumstances happens unconsciously. This makes it seem as if circumstances cause your feelings, behavior, and what you attract into your life. When this happens, it seems as if you are the result of external causes over which you have no control.

Happy people, however, even if they can't see how, know they're creating whatever is happening. They take responsibility.

Another characteristic of happy people is that their actions are the result of the possibilities they see. Where the unhappy person sees a challenge as impossible, the happy person sees what is possible. And, by focusing on what is possible, happy people make those possibilities come true.

A third characteristic of happy, successful people: They focus their minds on what they want and keep their minds off what they do not want.

Take prosperity, for instance. You could focus on not being poor, or you could focus on being rich. That is, you could make a mental picture of poverty, wanting to avoid it, or you could create a picture of being wealthy, wanting to move toward it.

In both cases, the intention is the same, but your brain doesn't care about your intentions. It just sees the literal content of the picture. When you focus on riches, it thinks you want riches and motivates you to see opportunities, find resources and take action to be rich.

When you focus on not being poor, your brain sees a picture of being poor and motivates you to see opportunities, find resources and take action...to be poor.

Most people focus on what they want to avoid without realizing the consequences. When they get what they didn't want, they assume they didn't focus hard enough and redouble their efforts. This creates even more of what they don't want, which creates more frustration.

The other penalty for focusing on what you don't want is that you feel bad. In fact, all bad feelings and negative outcomes are the result of focusing on what you do not want. Instead of unconsciously and automatically focusing on what you don't want, consciously and intentionally focus on what you do want. When you do this, you instantly begin to create it, and you instantly feel good.

The final characteristic: Happy people are consciously aware. As a result, their brains are less likely to run on automatic, creating internal states and external outcomes they did not intend and do not want.

First, become more consciously aware through meditation. Though traditional meditation is very beneficial, at Centerpointe Research Institute we use an audio technology called Holosync to create deep, meditative states, literally at the push of a button. This greatly accelerates the meditation process and allows you to create increased conscious awareness very quickly.

Second, investigate your own beliefs, values, ways of filtering information, strategies for decision making, motivations and other internal processes. Centerpointe's Life Principles Integration Process is a structured way of investigating and changing these internal processes, allowing you to take charge of how you create your internal and external results.

There is a price to pay to live the life you love. But paying it is a joyful enterprise that will benefit you for the rest of your life. You create your reality, so learn to focus your mind on what you want, and increase your conscious awareness through meditation and self-inquiry.

The life you love is waiting for you!

Bill Harris

What a Wake Up Moment!
Guy T. Insull

Mine was an incredible and magical wake up moment. I had been sitting in silence, staring out the window at a dark night sky. My mind was wandering peacefully.

I had just finished recording a series of personal development CDs and was loosely thinking about how to go about marketing them. That's when an incredible idea hit me. It was like the sun had exploded in its high noon position at the same time a choir reached its crescendo in my head. I know that sounds very theatrical, but it really was a very powerful moment. I've heard people talk about "flashes of inspiration" and I have always considered the phrase to be simply a figure of speech, but I can testify that "flashes of inspiration" are exactly what they say they are.

It's like when you suddenly recognize your destiny and you realize that—perhaps for the first time in your life—you truly know where you are going and what your life is all about. You can't help but experience it as a powerful jolt.

When that hits you and you can see a complete and undeniable idea laid out in front of you, it is like being hit by a lightning bolt. For a moment, as the lightning strikes, you can see the vision with perfect clarity. Then, even though the light is gone, the knowledge stays with you. The memory remains as clear as day and nothing will ever be the same again.

I have experienced that moment, and that is when *Champions Club* was born.

The vision that was so clearly etched in my mind was to create an online global community where like-minded individuals could come together to support mutual personal growth and development. That by acting as one, we really can make meaningful and positive changes in the world around us.

In creating *Champions Club,* I found two things. I not only found a great marketing strategy, I found something far more important than that as well—something more profound and much more valuable. I discovered something I hadn't even realized I was looking for. That something was the chance to make a difference—to do something worthwhile and good in the world—and that moment has transformed my life.

Each morning I wake up now with a purpose. I have something to do that makes my life more worthwhile than it has ever been. It's not about making money, although that is nice. It's about taking steps and supporting others in taking their own steps toward making a better world.

I get to communicate with people from around the world who are reaching for their dreams. From time to time I am even fortunate enough to be involved in their success.

I know when I go to bed each night that something I have done or have been able to share has helped someone make his or her own life a little better.

I believe if we all take care of our little bit of the planet and help to support those around us, then the world will become a better place. That makes me happy.

Through *Champions Club* and its developing community, I communicate with people who have great knowledge and wisdom. They share this with me and with each other, and we all benefit.

It's a simple philosophy: We can learn and develop more together than we can alone. By sharing knowledge, we help each other grow.

I have learned a great deal from exceptional individuals such as Stephen Covey, Brian Tracy and Vic Johnson—all three are worth Googling if you don't yet know who they are—and from many other remarkable people, including John Meredith, my brother Mark and my father.

Everybody has something to contribute, and in their own way, everybody is a real life champion. Together we find ways of improving each other's lives.

I'm interested in global development through personal development. That is, by facilitating personal development in the individual, I believe together we can change the world. If that sounds crazy—and some might say it does—think about it.

I recently learned that in some parts of the world children suffer from a disease that makes them blind. It would cost just 30 cents to fix—less than a third of the price of a bar of chocolate. One of the things *Champions Club* can do is encourage each member to donate 30 cents to help pay for the medicine so desperately needed by these children. When a million *Champions Club* members join forces to tackle a problem as basic as this, we truly can make a difference.

While helping to make an impact in another human being's life, every member of *Champions Club* is also able to benefit on a personal level because of the community input and valuable personal development information available through the *Champions Club* Web site.

In my world, all deals have to be "win-win" deals. That means everybody must benefit more than they would reasonably expect to for me to support it. This philosophy works because in *Champions Club* we all benefit from the massive resources produced by a lot of people, each putting in a little of his or her own.

Someone's contribution might be as simple as a valuable piece of advice that a thousand people can benefit from, so that thousand can make their part of the world a little better. It might just be that 30 cents. Of course, I probably don't have to spell out the impact a thousand people can have by enabling a thousand children to see in the world they live in. But in case I do, imagine the valuable contribution those kids can make to their communities with sight versus the challenge they might represent without it. Imagine, also, the improved quality of life each child would enjoy because of the 30 cents donated by a *Champions Club* member. Imagine how many people those one thousand kids could help and influence throughout *their* lives.

The *Champions Club Global Community* is growing. Every day, more and more people are finding us and joining up. They are inspired by what they find and excited by the power to do good.

We all want to leave a positive legacy when we go. We all want to be the best we can be in our own lives. For the first time in my life, I have found a way I can truly meet those two incredibly important needs. I am a better person because of *Champions Club,* and I do make a difference in the world because of the good I can do through it.

My wake up moment was a clear vision of how to bring together a lot of people looking to achieve positive things in their own lives and to make a difference on a global scale.

The lesson I can share is this: In isolation we achieve very little. Together we can change the world.

Guy T. Insull

WAKE UP AND LIVE!
Heidi Wright

I started my career as a California Highway Patrol Officer. During my tenure, my patrol car was crashed into, I was beaten by criminals, shot at twice and had a contract put out on my life. Many cannot understand it, but it was a dream job for me. During this time I began actively—though secretly—studying intuition and I used it to keep me safe while working.

I became certified as a drug recognition expert and focused on drug arrests. During one 12-month period, I made more felony arrests than the entire swing shift put together. I was a field training officer, training officers who trained new officers fresh from the academy. I also specialized in investigating accidents with fatalities, locating and documenting the on-scene evidence and drawing factual diagrams. I even had the camera crew from one of the first Fox reality shows, "Real Stories of the Highway Patrol," ride with me on four occasions, and was featured on the show numerous times. After nine years on the job, I was chosen as Officer of the Year by my peers and was awarded the American Legion Medal of Valor. My career was well under way. I had earned the respect of my fellow officers, and I was looking forward to many more years.

However, after more than 13 years with the CHP, I retired when an on-duty injury ended my career. I had intended to work for at least 30 years before retiring, but I found myself disabled, displaced and wondering, "What do I do now?" As I sat staring into space in my orthopedic surgeon's office near Mt. Shasta, California, numbly listening to him talk about my retirement, I was overcome deep down with fear. I already knew that after two surgeries and a year of physi-cal therapy, I could not do the job with my broken body, but finally hearing it out loud was like being told my dog had been hit by a car and killed. As my husband and I walked to the car after leaving the doctor's office, I suddenly broke down in tears, and he held me close. We stood embracing in the paved parking lot, surrounded by the pine trees, feeling the cool wind on our faces. He said to me, "You had to know this would happen." I was able to speak through my tears, and the truth escaped my lips before I could recognize it. I told my husband that I was crying because I was afraid I would never be as good at doing anything else as I had been at being an officer.

Retirement allowed me to pursue interests I never would have other-wise. I was able to teach my son to read—something I consider one of my greatest achievements—and was able to focus on metaphysics, meditation and animals.

While I was still grieving the loss of my career, my father passed away suddenly. Once again, I took stock of my life and the time I had been allotted. With my husband's encouragement, I bought my first horse. I quickly grew to love this horse, even though I learned the hard way that he had obviously been abused. We learned to trust each other and I learned to ride. But as time went on, my friend developed some issues. I knew it would sound a bit crazy if I told anyone I was inter-ested in psychic abilities, but I found an animal communicator and hired her to meet with my horse. She told me at least six things she could not have known that were validated. She also recommended a book to me, *Straight From the Horse's Mouth* by Amelia Kinkade. I went right out and bought the book about animal communication and was so enchanted I read it cover to cover. After an Internet search for the author, I found her Web site. I also saw that she would be teaching a workshop in my area in six weeks. This gave me just enough time to save the money for the workshop. I wanted so badly to learn how to communicate with animals, specifically my horse.

The workshop took place in the office of a veterinarian in Redding, California. I saw this beautiful, petite woman begin to teach, and I hung on her every word. The time came during the workshop to practice our animal communication skills. Somehow, some way, I was getting information from animals that was verified by their owners. Then I did it again and again. By the end of the second day, Amelia, whom I am now pleased to call my friend, took me by the hand and told me that she thought I was ready to become a professional animal communicator, and she wanted to start sending me referrals. I stood there with my mouth gaping open and vacantly replied, "Okay." Although my fears crept in, I decided to trust the advice of this best-selling author and celebrated psychic.

A few years later, some of my experiences with animals were included in her second book, *The Language of Miracles*. A year later, after a three-hour, on-camera interview, screen test and a test of my abilities, I was offered a job as an animal communicator for a hit television show in Japan. Since then, I have worked with animals and their owners from 19 countries around the globe. My television contract has been renewed, ratings for the segments are high and my producer is talking about the years to come as well as a book deal. My articles have been published internationally and I now teach my own workshops.

I became disabled for a reason. I found animal communication and the right teacher for a reason. All I had to do was trust that the reason was there, and then trust the advice of others when my fears crept in and I did not trust myself. Trust may be the most difficult thing to do, but it is the most empowering.

Heidi Wright

THE RESURRECTION OF THE DEAD
Orna Rav-Hon

My spiritual awakening began one Saturday morning, in early 2000, as I was sitting on the floor of my living room with a group of people who practiced Sidha Yoga, meaning "the yoga of the saints."

I was exhausted—absolutely washed out. The day before, I had held the last installment in a series of cultural meetings I used to run and produce. The last meeting was with the former prime minister and the current president of Israel, Mr. Shimon Peres.

I had done a lot of things in my life, but I didn't believe in myself or in my power. I felt blocked.

The Edge of Vanishing
Only my poems are left as refuge
In the area
That frames all the windows.
But you on the glass ceiling
Are blocked
With any effort to take off
To the edge of vanishing
The edge of the soul's transcendence.

I was always on the brink of some ominous cliff. I was constantly wandering, somnambulant, from the middle to the edge, trying to create some order in my life.

The light was always there, but I didn't notice. I was haunted by old

traumas that darkened my days and flooded me with unbearable pain
and many bad memories.

Impertinent Light-hour
How could I have forgotten
that yellow-scented hour.
The ring of an ancient silence
still cuts me
like a knife—
impertinent light-hour.
How could I have forgotten
its return as steel
ripping and exposing
my insides to the wind.

When I was very young, my mother left. I was sure she was gone for
good, and losing her was paralyzing. I felt a sharp pain in the right
side of my body, as if a big black hole were gaping there and swal-
lowing all my seconds, minutes and hours, refusing to stop.

My mother was a teacher, a very devoted teacher. I used to envy her
pupils because she was busy all the time. She was like a honeybee,
trying to navigate her life between obstacles. I remember her falling
asleep on the kitchen table on the piles of the notebooks that she had
to fix. My heart yearned for her, full of compassion.

When You Were Gone
To my mother:

When you were gone
I went out to the street.

Shops were shut.
Traffic lights endlessly flicked.
People walked in the streets,
Faces sealed.

And in the train I clasped a child
And another one
And the trees were going
Going and gone,
Going, gone…

The sadness was a constant lodger in our home. We used to live together with my grandfather and my grandmother, who had managed to escape from Lithuania before World War II, when the huge waves of anti-Semitism began to rise.

My grandmother raised me while my mother worked. I remember her sorrow like a solid stone in my heart. She used to cry almost all the time about her seven sisters who were killed in the Holocaust together with all their families.

My grandfather lost his beloved brother who was killed by Stalin in Russia. But he was a religious man, and his belief in God caused his bright blue eyes to sparkle with joy. This sparkle saved my life because I cherished it in my heart during tough times. In addition to the former troubles, my uncle was taken prisoner in the war between Israel and the Muslim countries. He was a captive for one long year—a year that marked our family with dark signs of deep sorrow.

Later on, my beloved and handsome brother, a pilot in the Israeli Army, crashed with his airplane and was severely wounded.

All those things created a blockage of sorrow and rage that burdened my heart to such an extent that I wished to die. I just couldn't see the beauty of life. I felt as if a big stone were pulling me down to the dark silence of death.

But that Saturday morning in yoga, my life changed forever. The sparkle of God that was hidden, asleep in the bottom of my heart, livened up.

As I was sitting, I saw all the people standing up and singing enthusiastically. They gestured for me to get up as they had, but this was the first time I participated in that ritual and didn't understand the meaning of their actions. I told them, "This is my home and in my home I'll do whatever I want." I continued sitting without understanding what they were singing because it was in Sanskrit.

Suddenly, I felt a current of white light showering me from the inside, head to toe.

I had never felt something like that before. It was a flash of light that lasted only a second, but it was immense. It felt as if it lasted forever and ever. I felt a great joy and a great inner tranquility, I was totally protected—as if I were really in Heaven on Earth.

Heaven on Earth
Mingling of sun and smoke.
Coffee aroma
as always
wide open
misty
with a long, long siren.

Breathe,
take in this beauty.
It's like ascending to the heavens.

I knew that I had a mission.

I knew that my mission was to spread the light using the Hebrew language, the language of the Tora, the language of the Bible, the language that was discovered by Abraham the patriarch. I would use the language that has the power to transmit our consciousness from the material dimension to the spiritual dimension.

I should do this together while working on myself constantly, in order to become a better person, a happier person, a person who can create his inner joy and his own destiny. If everybody will work on himself from the inside and change himself for the best, we will be able to change the world.

I am working hard to purify my heart. I know and feel that it is possible. As a result of this realization, I started learning Kabbalah and grew closer to my heritage of Judaism.

My life became more illuminated. As I feel absolute certainty in the power of the Creator, I can perform any task with greater self-confidence and self-esteem and, therefore, with greater success.

I know the power of the One—the power of unity. If every one of us will purify himself, all the world will be purified and change for the best.

Orna Rav-Hon

The poems in this story are taken from the books:
Like The Phoenix (Dvir, Israel)
Touch Of Stars (Ma'ariv, Israel)
Blessed Me, For Making Myself a Woman (Bitan, Israel)
Firebird (Cross-Cultural Communications, NY, USA)

The poems were translated from Hebrew by the author, Orna Rav-Hon; Jessica Cohen; Stanley H. Barkan; Karen Alkalay-Gut; and Riva Rubin.

FROM EMPOWERMENT TO INPOWERMENT
Edward A. Rodriguez

Have you ever had an experience so powerful it marked your life in such a way that you would never be the same again? This happened to me when I was 14 years old. I was looking for something to read, and this time, I decided to pick up a book I had seen many times in my house, but had never sufficiently attracted my attention.

What a discovery! Imagine, for a moment, a 14-year-old boy receiving a new toy, but not one you would buy with money. Was this a coincidence? Was this meant to be? You see, my mother was very young when I was born and it seemed that the teachings from this book came from the father I never had.

I was in awe by the end of the third page! At that age, I could not believe there were books that would teach you how to create your own future and how to become like those you admire.

The title of the book was *Your Erroneous Zones* by Dr. Wayne W. Dyer.

I must say the chapters titled, "How to Take Charge of My Life," and, "I Don't Need Their Approval," made me hungry for more. There was a strong chain reaction that moved me to search for more books from the same author and on self-development in general. I was "empowered" and my life would never be the same.

I started reading about psychology, parapsychology, Transactional Analysis, Neuro-Lingustic Programming and anything that crossed my hands on human achievement. I even explored different religions in search for answers, and three years later, I was literally investing everything I earned on my first job into books and seminars. I was on a quest for knowledge!

The first workshop I ever attended was called, "How to Project Yourself Professionally." I must admit that with such a title and being only 17, I even asked myself, "What am I doing here?" but then the answer became apparent. The speaker exerted a noticeable influence on the audience and a magical effect upon me. Right there, I decided that when I grew up, I wanted to be a motivational speaker. A dream was born.

But the magic ended when I came to the United States. At the age of 19, I left the Dominican Republic (my country of birth) and moved to New York. I allowed myself to get distracted with the "high speed" life of this big city. I got caught up with the outer world and wanted to fit in and become like everyone else.

I became too comfortable and put aside my dream until I retired. I even discouraged myself from reading other books written by Dr. Dyer because I felt his teachings were turning too spiritual for my taste at that time. It all looked like the noise of my youth was louder than the beat of passion in my heart. Deep inside I still knew that if I continued like this, one day I was going to die with my book unwritten, my song unsung and my dream unrealized.

Many years later, things were about to change. One day I was watching a program on TV where Dr. Dyer was being featured. I decided to give myself the opportunity to pay attention with my heart and not with my mind. His words once again truly inspired me and for the first time in my life, I understood the real meaning of spirituality. I had been wrong for so long because I thought it had to do with merely being religious.

He asked the proverbial question, "What would you be doing if you knew you could not fail?" That was it, just like being hit with a rock! Have you ever heard something countless times, but one day, you listened with your heart and it made all the difference? His whole message impacted me so much that I felt like the prodigal son returning back to his father.

I recommitted myself to my lifelong dream of becoming a motivational speaker, but now, not at retirement age as I had once thought. I immediately felt a tremendous amount of energy, motivation and clarity. I understood what the poets and writers meant when they referred to "lighting the fire within." It all had to do with aligning my dream with my passion and purpose, not when it would be convenient, but now.

This was the time when I became what I call "In-Powered!" You see, at 35, I was already very successful in the businesses I had created. I was driving luxury cars and had built the home of my dreams in the mountains where I now live with my wonderful wife and two kids. Everything I had heard and read about success before empowered me to work and acquire things, but I did not feel fulfilled. Even though I had the toys, vacations and the lifestyle I wanted, part of me felt empty inside and disconnected with my true self. There had to be more to life than that.

I knew that realizing my dreams someday was a possibility, but knowing that at an intellectual level was not enough. I needed to align my passion and my purpose with my thoughts, feelings and actions…that's the essence of *InPowerment*: connecting yourself to your own greatness and creating fulfilling and sustainable results in your life.

From that moment on, I was totally transformed. I let go of the crazy idea of waiting until retirement to start living my dream, and now this dream is driving me from within.

I believe all of us have the power to change our lives, but we often fail to be attentive. We become blind to our uniqueness, to our talents and to our calling.

My experience at age 14 not only changed my life, but is now positively affecting the lives of thousands of people around the world, as I present them with my message of *InPowerment*. If you want to be fulfilled, start living your dreams now. God is waiting for you. The world is waiting for you. Your life is waiting for you.

If you are not answering your calling at this time, you are depriving yourself of the satisfaction of being fulfilled. The lives of those you were meant to touch with the uniqueness of your existence will miss out.

When your dream knocks on your door and you feel empowered, make sure you listen to your conscience, follow your heart and connect it to your inner purpose and passion. You will become *InPowered* and your life will never be the same again.

Little did I know when I was 14 that I would be co-authoring this book with Dr. Wayne Dyer, the person responsible for my beginning on this wonderful journey of...*InPowerment*.

Edward A. Rodriguez

THREE WORDS
Gary Addams

"If I knew I was going to live this long, I would have taken better care of myself."—Mickey Mantle

You have diabetes!

In 2006, when I was 64, my doctor told me I was a type II diabetic. "You have diabetes," he said. Those three words were devastating to me. The doctor continued talking for another 10 minutes, but all I could hear were those words echoing in my head. In previous visits, my doctor suggested I was a pre-diabetic but offered no advice other than to lose weight and exercise. There was no urgency or threat of imminent doom, and no further discussion about what having diabetes really meant. Despite the standard brevity of these medical visits, I heard no description of the inevitable pain and suffering that diabetes could bring if I did not change my diet and lifestyle. All of the discussions were very professional, friendly and conducted in a timely manner. Meanwhile, my weight ballooned to 280 pounds and my A1C level was hovering at a high nine. (A1C is a test that gives an average 90-day picture of your blood sugar levels. So, if you try to impress the doctor by staying on your diet the 24 to 48 hours beforehand to get a good blood sugar reading, the doctor will know. It's hard to make it look good if you haven't been following the rules.) I was a mess.

I decided to become my own advocate. I studied everything I could get my hands on. I spoke to other diabetics who were making progress in their health and found inspiration online and through endless reading. Motivated by the possibility that this disease didn't have to be a death sentence, I made changes in my diet and lifestyle. I exercised regularly, lowered my saturated fat, decreased the meats in my diet and ate enough vegetables to make my mother proud. I developed a taste for whole grains and found fruit to satisfy my sweet urges. I have lost 55 pounds with this regimen. My A1C is now below six. I have no need for medication and my cholesterol is lower than it has been in 30 years. One of the best parts is that my doctor is amazed. Compared to where I was two years ago, I have transformed my health.

What Can We Do?

There are many things we diabetics can do to slow, halt and even reverse diabetes. To make these improvements we need practical, hard-hitting information that's easy to understand and produces proven results. We need to remember that on a daily basis we have more control over our health than we previously thought, and we need to discover new ways to remain hopeful, inspired and on the right path.

I created a Web club for diabetics and their family members who are willing to take the next step in improving their health. Research has proven that a balanced, whole food diet, along with exercise, reduced stress and daily monitoring of blood glucose levels are the winning ingredients to overcoming this potentially debilitating disease.

The medical community and their health organizations seem to share the opinion that diabetics are not capable of doing these things consistently. They attempt to make up for our perceived inability to do what's best for ourselves by advising us to remain on medication in order to keep our blood sugar levels regular and to delay life-threatening symptoms. But let me tell you something you probably already know—diabetes is a merciless, relentless and equal opportunity debilitator. Diabetes can also make all of our other illnesses much more severe. It affects every system in our body and if left unchecked, diabetes will shorten our lives, give us crippling misery and eat up every last cent we have with treatments—treatments with potentially harmful side effects to which you become dependent.

It has become abundantly clear to me: Real healthcare begins with self-care.

The Disaster Addiction

We diabetics are in a battle no different than the one fought by recovering alcoholics, smokers and drug addicts. We must constantly be on guard, mindful about our sugar levels, motivated to keep our circulation moving and precise about medication measurements. In the moments when we forget, we risk the enemies advancing upon us. Any enemy advance forces us to work twice as hard to keep the opponent at bay. But, as long as we're feeding its needs—poor nutrition and inactivity—it remains relentlessly progressive. Too often we discover that the battle would have been much easier to fight if we were more aware of the early warning signs and had marshaled the proper strategies to overcome this onslaught.

Now, here's the good news. If you are a diabetic, you can *still* be in control. You can have a positive and transformative influence on the quality of the rest of your life. You can rediscover the peace of mind to know that with a little effort, you don't have to end as a statistic. Each change you make guides you to the next. Your belief and conviction strengthen with the knowledge and experience that you *can* make a difference.

Here's to your health!

Gary Addams

OVERCOMING ADVERSITY WHILE KEEPING YOUR COOL
Brian Tracy

You will have to deal with countless problems and difficulties throughout your life. They never end. The only question is "How good are you when it comes to overcoming the inevitable adversities?"

What are you made of? What are you *really* made of? When push comes to shove, when the rubber meets the road, when the chips are down, what lies at the very core of your character?

You learn what you can really handle only when things go wrong and you stumble, head over heels, by some adversity or setback that hits you like a Mack truck. Since your behaviors on the outside are the real indicators of who you are on the inside, only by observing how you behave when things go wrong can you tell what you really have inside of you.

Let's make one thing clear right now: Life is a continuous succession of both small and large problems. They never end. As soon as you get control of one situation, you are hit by another. Life is a process consisting of two steps forward and one step back. Becoming successful makes you no different. When you become a great success, you simply exchange one type of problem for another. Before the success, you had small problems with limited consequences; now you have large problems with enormous consequences. No matter how smart, clever and careful you are, you'll face challenges, difficulties and sometimes heartbreaking adversities every day, week and month of your life. But thank Heaven for that! You couldn't possibly have become the person you are today if you had not contended with adversity on your way up. Only by contending with challenges that seem beyond your strength at the moment can you grow more surely toward the stars.

The starting point in dealing with any difficulty is to simply relax. Clear your mind. Get yourself into a state where you're calm, cool and in full control of your emotions and senses. Back off mentally and become as objective as possible. Step back and look at the problem with a certain amount of detachment, as if it were happening to someone else. When you can analyze your adversities clearly, you will sometimes see opportunities to turn them to your best advantage.

Remember, too, that you are never given a problem too big for you to handle. Whatever problems or adversities you face, you have within you the resources to deal with them. You have the creative ability to find a solution to your problem. You have within you, right now, everything you need to deal with whatever the world will throw at you.

Here are three steps you can use immediately to put these ideas into action.

First, treat every problem or difficulty as if it were a test to see how capable and competent you are. Look for ways to grow and benefit, to pass the test with high marks.

Second, stay calm no matter what. The longer you can stay calm and relaxed, the better decisions you can make and the faster you will come out of your difficulty.

Third, ask other people who have had the same problem for their advice. Don't try to solve it all by yourself.

No matter what problem you have, say to yourself, "This, too, shall pass."

Brian Tracy

TO THE TOP, ASPIRING TO EXCELLENCE
Peter R. Thurin

My name is Peter Thurin and I'm based in Melbourne, Australia, but currently holidaying beside the beach many miles north in one of Australia's glamorous holiday destinations, Noosa. I'm sitting on my balcony overlooking the ocean, thinking how incredibly lucky I am to be here, to be who I am and to be who I'm going to be!

I am one person who is truly living the life he loves! But this wasn't always so. I'm here today because of a series of life-changing decisions—pivotal moments that defined my life. All of us are where our choices have taken us, whether we have made good decisions or bad. My hope is that my story might help you make choices that will lead you to live the life you love.

I am now a public speaker, facilitator, business consultant, mentor and coach through my company, Blackbelt in Excellence. In this role, I have the amazingly good fortune to travel the world. Before this, I was a pharmacist and businessman. I have a family—a wonderful wife, two great boys and a beautiful daughter. I love sports and coached junior football for many years. I represented Australia in tennis when I was young, but when I was 36, I made a big decision. That's where it all began.

I decided to do something I had always wanted to do but had never gotten around to. I had that procrastination syndrome and was always putting things off. I decided to get a black belt in Tae Kwon Do before I turned 40. Today, I am the holder of a third dan black-belt.

What I find extraordinary is that many people I speak to think, "WOW!" but when I ask them questions about their own life journeys, they tell me stories that blow me away—absolutely inspirational stuff. We often take for granted our own endeavors but then marvel at what others achieve.

I, myself, am inspired by a vast array of things, from sunsets to great movies, to my unbelievable wife and kids. Inspiration is everywhere—all the time and in the most everyday moments. For example, in my book, *Be the Best You Can Be,* I tell the story of my daughter Mel and her fierce desire to own a dog when she was 6. I mean, she *really* wanted one! Her whole life revolved around getting a dog. The problem was I was not a big fan of them, but she badgered me—begged, pleaded, cajoled. She argued strongly for the fabulous benefits of dog ownership. I was unmoved.

Then, one day I went to the mailbox and was more than a little surprised. Addressed to me was a letter, but not just any letter. This one was from GOD! Written in a surprisingly childish hand from the Almighty, the letter explained to me how very important it was for my daughter, Mel, to have a dog. The signature at the end said, "God."

Guess what? We got a dog! Mel taught me you can have anything you want if you're prepared to do whatever it takes and never give up. When I think I have exhausted all of my options, I remember my possibilities and opportunities are endless. In addition, Mel has also taught me the joy of having a pet. I now seriously love our dog, Ruffi!

That "I can do anything" attitude took me through a series of early-morning training sessions, gutbusting workouts, physical punishment, pulled muscles and broken bones, as I worked relentlessly toward that elusive Tae Kwon Do black belt, but I finally got it. I did it. You can imagine how empowered and overjoyed I felt when I finally wrapped that coveted black belt around my waist.

It was then that I made another decision. Why stop at just one? After all, I had already proven I could do anything I set my mind to. So, after having established a very successful pharmacy in a highly competitive area of Melbourne, I sold my thriving business and began to do what I had always really wanted to do. This is what I mean when I tell you I really do live the life I love now. I left the pharmacy behind and established Blackbelt in Excellence, with the sole aim of empowering others to take those small steps—one color at a time and one belt at a time, to use the martial arts metaphor—toward excellence in whatever they choose.

Another of my life's pivotal moments came when my son, Jamie, was a kid. I was asked to coach his under-9 football team. Jamie was so excited at the thought of his dad coaching him and his mates. However, he wasn't as excited as I was when they won the under-14 premiership! It was also with Jamie that I took up martial arts when he was only six. It was a journey we took together, laughing and encouraging each other every step of the way. As a father, I was so proud the day he received his black belt.

The extraordinary thing is that these two activities, coaching and martial arts, are the basis of my professional life today. Jamie and my other son Matt have been enormous catalysts in bringing about Blackbelt in Excellence.

You know, we really don't need to look too far for inspiration. There are inspirational stories all around us. I hear them at every seminar and every conference. People turn unhealthy lifestyles into healthy lifestyles. They build strong relationships where once there were none. People write books even though they failed English in school. Others move with their families to a completely foreign land and start new lives.

What about you? How can you be the best you can be? Ask yourself these powerful questions:
What new skills would I need?
Do I need new knowledge?
Whom else would I need on my team?
What one step could I take right now to move me in that direction?
Who could I possibly inspire by believing in them?
Who needs an arm around his shoulder?
Who needs to be encouraged? Supported? Listened to?

You see, inspiration works both ways. Be inspired, and be a source of inspiration. Do that, and you'll be "Living the Life You Love!"

Peter R. Thurin

LIFE IS AN ADVENTURE—DRAMA IS OPTIONAL!
Judee Ausnow

I was born to a wonderful mother who loved my sister and me very much. Unfortunately, she married a man who drank excessively and they both became alcoholics—drinking was an acceptable pastime in the mid 1940s. Today, I know that experience was no "accident." I was so embarrassed by my mom's and stepfather's behavior that I knew when I became a parent I would never subject my children to that embarrassment, feelings of unworthiness, and especially the *fear* of not knowing what to expect when they came home from school each day. I was too young to really get the "big picture" in those days, but I somehow *knew* the experience was creating a strength deep within me that would serve me throughout my entire life. I was creating a passion within to want a better life for myself than the one I was experiencing in my own home. I know today, beginning life in this environment was the best thing that could have happened to me—it was the beginning of the creation of "the passion within me" to want a better life for myself and others.

When I look back on my life in five-year segments, it is clear to me that each step along the way has led to the next experience. Without the experiences I've had in my life, I would not be the person I am today. *Life is experiences!* It's what we do with those experiences that creates the life we live, and that's *our* choice.

Pretend your life is a book in progress and you are the author. Ask yourself what the completed chapters look like and how you want the next chapter to be. If you could create your life any way you choose, what would you change? What would you add to your life and what you take away from it? If the next chapter of your life could be any way you wanted it to be, if you truly were the author of your own life—of your next experience—what would it be like?

I have learned that the secret to having the life we want is created by our thoughts. When you ask people what they want in life, they usually start telling you what they don't want. What they don't realize is that we get exactly what we focus on—and focusing our attention on what we *don't* want just creates more of what we don't want in our lives. Most of us have a hard time describing what we *do* want because our attention is focused on what we don't want. What if we started thinking about what we do want—really thinking about what would make us happy, what would make our *hearts smile*—and started putting our attention on that? Ahh…what then?

It has been said that even in the most complicated computers there are only three components: the *hard drive*, the *operating system*, and *the programs*. Scientists have described life as a consciousness computer that also has only three components; *our physical world* is the hard drive, *our consciousness* is the operating system, *our thoughts* are the programs. You don't change the hard drive on your computer to create something new, you change the programs. It is the same in life. If you want to create something new for yourself, you don't have to change your physical world, you simply change your thoughts. Changing your thoughts literally changes the experience you create in your life because your thoughts create your feelings and emotions—and your feelings and emotions have the power to make you feel really, really good, or really, really bad. It's difficult to believe sometimes, but the truth is that it's not what's happening around us that's making us unhappy, it's our reaction to it. I have learned that when I stop reacting and just pay attention to my feelings, amazing things start to happen and new experiences open up for me…it's just like magic!

One day, while sitting on the bleachers at the high school as my granddaughter participated in her cheerleading activities, I was observing a large group of teenagers who were waiting for the football game to begin. As I was listening to the *less than complimentary* comments that were being slung around by these kids who were supposed to be "friends," the idea was born of a "just the facts" book for teenagers—a guide to help them eliminate the everyday "drama" and find balance in their lives.

In my meditation the next morning I began asking God what I could do to help the kids and the words started to flow. I had heard many times over the years about "automatic writing," but had no idea what that really meant until I experienced it myself. The writing became so automatic that when I re-read the pages I was amazed at the information I had written. It was clear to me that writing this book was what I was meant to do. I was being given the opportunity of fulfilling my *purpose* and allowing the passion within me to help others. In thinking back, I realize there have been many times in my life that the "opportunity" has arisen to do something for others, but I wasn't really listening. This time I knew I needed to pay attention to the information I was being given, which resulted in the writing of my book, *Drama Is Optional: A Guide For Teens.* It was immediately clear to me that this was my passion.

Passion is really what life is all about. When we find our passion, our lives begin to change right before our eyes. My passion is to help make a difference in the lives of teens. I am literally "Living the Life I Love" when I'm sharing the "ideas" in *Drama Is Optional*—ideas that I have learned over the past 20 years from many great teachers in the field of self-improvement. I'm a firm believer that the only *original thought* is God's; everything else is what we allow ourselves to learn in life. I am amazed at all the information that's available to help us make our lives work. There are hundreds of books and CDs on almost every subject imaginable. If you ask people who you consider to have succeeded in their lives, they will almost always mention someone who influenced them along the way (for me, that person is Dr. Wayne W. Dyer). We all have teachers in our lives and, if we pay attention, they're not always who we expect them to be. Treat everyone you meet as the most important person you could meet each day—because you never know what you have to learn from them. Be open to new experiences and beware of feeling that you are an "expert" in anything. You cannot learn if you're convinced you already know! Really succeeding in life is not measured by how much money you make. It's measured by how much *joy* you bring to your life every day. So, find your passion and remember as you're doing it that *Drama is Optional.*

Judee Ausnow

P<small>ERSISTENCE</small>: M<small>Y</small> P<small>ATH TO</small> E<small>MPOWERMENT</small>
Venu

E mpowerment isn't a destination I've reached; it's an ongoing jour-ney for me.

I was born on a cold winter night in a small farm town in northern Wisconsin. My mother's body—my "home" for the last nine months—was host to multiple sclerosis, yet her constant loving example of kindness and her willingness to help others taught me not to give up in the face of adversity.

When money was tight, I saved my allowance and bought my own Brownie uniform. I was six years old and I learned not to depend on anyone for money or anything else. This lesson was one of the most motivating gifts from my childhood.

One of my major life lessons has come from being different. At a young age, I was different because I had a handicapped mother and a different religion—I was the only Jewish girl in a school of a thou-sand students. Still, I was embraced and chosen Outstanding Senior Woman. My religion continued to challenge me in college, but I was selected as one of four outstanding senior women at the University of Wisconsin out of more than 40,000 students. I always followed my mom's example of constantly reaching for a higher goal.

My career in advertising presented the challenge of being both a woman and a Jewish person in a Midwest advertising community that embraced neither. I started out as an apprentice art director and I'd been promoted to vice president/creative director by the time I formed my own company. I had won every major award in the industry, spoken on television and on university panels, had judged award shows and my work has been published in national and international books and magazines. However, something was missing.

I didn't know what was wrong. I'd done everything I thought would fulfill me. I'd succeeded in the world, was happily married and had a loving family. Yet, although I could not name it at the time, I was not empowered; my life was not truly in my control.

Suddenly, my personal life changed cataclysmically. My marriage fell apart and I ran away from home to Esalen in Big Sur, California. There, I met a photographer who, along with his roommates, was preparing for "Conversations with Bucky." Bucky was, of course, Buckminster Fuller, one of the key innovators of the 20th century. I helped the group build models of Bucky's famed tetrahedron for the events. At the final event, Bucky had each of us look under our seats. We discovered a piece of cardboard with a map of the world. It was a small globe made of tetrahedrons (triangles).

This view of the Earth was part of a 50-year mission. At the age of 33, Bucky's child was born. He made a 50-year contract with himself to use his gifts, no matter how small, to make "spaceship earth," as he called it, a better place. Now, his 50 years were up; he was passing on his commitment to each of us to continue the work.

This was my first real insight into a person who was working for a cause greater than himself. I felt his empowerment and he was passing his commitment on to each of us.

Soon, I was traveling around the world with my best friend, Geya. I'd said goodbye to my mother. The MS had imprisoned her in her own body. We both acknowledged she might die in my absence. She stated repeatedly that she wanted to die but couldn't. I asked three psychics why. They all said the same thing, "You keep her alive. Each time she begins to let go of life, you rush to her, bringing her back to life. She lives off your energy. Leave! Go so far you can't come back and she'll let go." She had always told me she lived off my energy.

So, I went on a trip around the world to help her let go. It was a difficult goodbye. She died on my birthday; I was visiting a guru at an ashram in India. The guru told me, "Always follow your heart." I'd been given permission in a handwritten note from the wisest person I knew! This was a very empowering step toward finding myself and embracing spirituality instead of religion.

My father died the following year. As if the universe were compensating for my loneliness, I fell in love with Sam. Following my heart, I "dropped out," moved to California and, eventually, we married. Using my life savings to finance myself, I went broke and so did Sam, which brought more lessons in persistence and not giving up.

Sam soon opened a successful company. My own business successes allowed me to become an entrepreneur, working on my own projects. I wrote and illustrated a book titled, *Rainbow Stress Reduction: Play Your Stress Away with Colorful Healing Art and Stress Reducing Games.*

Success took on new meaning for me. The National Hospice Bereavement Group used the book with children who were in shock and unable to communicate after the loss of a parent. The children and caregivers learned to communicate from concepts in the book. Cigna used it as a textbook for employees. Universities used it, too. These unexpected surprises made the book an amazing success.

When I was ready to promote the book, I became too ill to get out of bed. I gave my life over to a higher power, stating, "I've done the best I can. I give my life to you and am ready to do your work. Please make what you want me to do really obvious so I don't miss it." My journey to empowerment included giving my power to a higher source.

Answers didn't come quickly, but they did come. I went to Mexico to an Australian cancer specialist. Everyone thought I was crazy. I didn't listen, went anyway, recovered physically and had taken another step toward empowerment.

A few years later, my beloved soul mate, Sam, was diagnosed with cancer. He died six weeks later, and Geya moved in for weeks at a time.

Geya and Sam were my "bookends," my nearest and dearest, my immediate family. Then Geya died. They'd both crossed over and I was *totally* alone. My earlier pattern of loss had repeated itself.

I discovered that my investment firm was losing my money. "Enough!" I said. I moved the money, lived on it, formed a team and began to invest myself.

Then, everything began to turn around. Money isn't empowerment, but taking responsibility can be.

Real empowerment hasn't come from becoming more successful in the world or accumulating more. Empowerment has come from giving my life over to a power higher than myself, as well as losing everything and everyone and becoming totally self-responsible. Now I show up asking for guidance. I'm not attached to outcomes, but do whatever guidance asks of me.

This has led to using concepts introduced in *Rainbow Stress Reduction,* in a new form: TIME OUT® is a computer program aimed at using my gifts to make "spaceship earth" a better place. TIME OUTS are childhood-to-grave, computerized, interactive learning programs for specific age groups, cultures and different ways of learning. The goal is to help kids by addressing two main issues in education: bad behavior in schools and the expulsion rate.

The Yale University Child Study Center, found that "Pre-kindergarten students are expelled at a rate more than three times that of students in K-12." Just as I persist and don't give up, TIME OUT helps kids not to give up and get expelled from school because of behavioral problems. It helps kids and schools not give up on their paths to empowerment.

I found that we teach what we want to learn. So, day by day, I walk the path to self empowerment.

I'm not done yet. I'm still a work in progress.

Venu

MORE THAN A LIFETIME
Emanuela Bertozzini

The water is warm, running from my head to my toes and giving me the wonderful comfort of the first shower of the day. The familiar scent of the sandalwood soap gives me energy while I brush my skin ritualistically. I have a train to catch for a long trip to Turin, and I am planning to meet some very special people.

Traveling is always special to me. The movement of the train makes me feel like I'm in a cocoon, and a few minutes after departure, my mind starts to wander while memories resurface.

I have always believed in reincarnation, much to the despair of the nuns and family members who were trying to bring me up as a "good Catholic girl." And "good" I was, but I could never accept beliefs that did not touch my heart and mind. Instead, I always believed in energy—personal and mind energy—and this has brought me through all of my life's events. I longed to understand energy, to use it for my own good and for the good of others.

It was during my training at BBSH that I discovered the wonderful world of past life regression. I decided to follow my inspiration and seek professional training in the field. Eventually, doors opened for me to be trained by Dr. Brian Weiss.

I now understand that "the secret" was in my actions as I began my professional life with all of the enthusiasm and passion I had. I could then change my life and help others to change theirs while overcoming problems and difficult issues. The struggle was mostly with my ego, but my training and goodwill helped whenever it surfaced.

One of the most difficult cases I had was a 32-year-old woman who was afflicted with bulimia and in early menopause. My practice is in central Italy, but she came to me from the north, full of determination and motivation. I couldn't suggest she change doctors, so I relied on my skills and her willpower. This was difficult for me in the beginning—responsibility and fear of failure were obstacles—but I decided to take it one step at a time.

The synergy of our efforts worked perfectly, and a few days after the first session, the bulimia had been defeated. Her determination was stronger, as was my desire to help her. Dramatic changes took place in her life, from her figure to her love life to her desire to have a family. She had a long love story not yet realized because of her health problems and lack of self-esteem, but she now felt ready to face the challenge and was confident in the future.

Six months later, she was pregnant, and in due time, gave birth to a healthy baby boy! The faith she had in life and the passion she put in her efforts made the impossible possible. I was impressed. I wondered, "What were the ingredients—or better—what were the proportions of the ingredients for this successful recipe?"

This change and my client's new choices helped her overcome more difficulties when, two years later, she gave birth to a baby girl with serious health problems. She knew that, despite the difficulties, her baby would make it.

I remained in her life, witnessing all of the challenges she overcame. At the same time, I worked on my own issues, feeling very grateful to the universe for all the support it gave us both.

My mind was wandering and remembering all these things when a glance through the train window brought me back to the present. My destination was approaching and a sense of anticipation surfaced in my heart.

I was sitting at one of the famous coffee shops when I saw my old client, Paula, and her toddlers. A giant wave of emotion swept over me when a smiling little boy came running up to hug me. In a fraction of a second, I had my arms around him. His little sister was still too shy to come forward. They looked bigger than their last picture.

We spent the rest of the afternoon enjoying ice cream and talking. The children were full of life, differing in everything but their common trait of determination. Paula was perfect in her role as a mother. She was understanding and loving, yet strong. Her experience and sufferings were just milestones in her life, as well as mine.

When we parted that evening, I brought back with me the children's smiles as hymns to life and to the universe that had made such a dream possible.

Time has passed since then and I visit Turin regularly. I enjoy my work and, if I sometimes encounter painful issues, the smiles of "my" children give me the strength and the stamina to go on.

Emanuela Bertozzini

THE "BIGGIES" I HAVE LEARNED IN THIS LIFETIME
Ian Hewitt

When offered the opportunity to be a co-author in this book with such esteemed writers, I was concerned that I wouldn't have anything worthwhile to add. Finally, I imagined I had been reincarnated and was reading this book for guidance upon my return to Earth. So, what follows are insights and lessons I have learned in this lifetime that I would like to pass on to you.

Master Mind Groups
When I returned to Perth, Australia, after 15 years of teaching English and doing business in Japan, I discovered my youngest brother had become very successful by promoting products that aid in stress relief and meditation techniques. He owned the lucrative Web site Meditate.com.au.

Although I'd been moderately successful in creating several of my own Web-based business ventures, we were not in the same league. When it came to creating cash flow, he was in front. So I asked him what his secret was and he simply replied, "Mentors and Master Mind groups."

If it worked for him, then it might work for me. I asked him to introduce me to these Master Mind groups and we began to go to wealth creation seminars around Australia.

Being an active participating member of Master Mind groups works.

The Penny Drops
First, let's define a "Master Mind group." In 1938, Napoleon Hill wrote in *Think and Grow Rich* that having a Master Mind group is essential for success.

"You who read this book will get the most out of it by putting into practice the Master Mind principle described in the book. This you can do (as others are doing so successfully) by forming a study club, consisting of any desired number of people who are friendly and harmonious."—Napoleon Hill

12-Step Programs: The Ultimate Master Mind Group
12-step recovery programs, (first implemented by Bill Wilson and Dr. Bob Smith of Alcoholics Anonymous), have empowered more people to radical change than any other process in the history of mankind.

What was discovered was that neither Bill nor Bob could stop drinking by themselves and they were nearing death. However, together with the same goal, they could achieve daily sobriety.

Nobody is certain how AA works, exactly, but it is undeniable that it has achieved incredible worldwide success. Now there are over 30 types of 12-step groups.

I guess it is quite obvious, really. If you wanted to climb a mountain, you would probably join a mountain climbing club. However, I have noticed that those with addiction problems often go to doctors and social workers before they finally try a 12-step program. If you are having any addiction problems, my advice is to go to one of these programs first. Only a person who has overcome a particular addiction can help others overcome it.

Gratitude
One of the important discoveries and precepts taught in 12-step programs is gratitude.

They discovered that it is impossible to have any negative emotions while feeling truly grateful. It's possible to feel excited and grateful, or relieved and grateful, but it's impossible to feel sad and grateful, or angry and grateful.

You can only experience positive emotions when you're honestly grateful for all the blessings in your life.

Most emotions are hard to control, but gratitude can actually be cultivated. Simply write down the things you are grateful for. Making a gratitude list often, and especially in times of acute stress, is certain to upgrade your life experience for the better.

It is now a well-known and documented spiritual law that you get more of what you are grateful for and less of what you take for granted.

If you want more of the good things in life and less of the worry, try the mantra, "I want what I have today and am very grateful." Say it over and over again until you believe it in your core.

Tips to a Superb Life

These are taken from the Internet and other sources. I do not do all of them all of the time, but I have found that all of the tips are very good for you.

1. Take a 10- to 30-minute walk every day and smile while you walk—it is the ultimate anti-depressant.
2. Sit in silence for at least 10 minutes each day.
3. Buy a TIVO (DVR), tape your late night shows for later viewing and get more sleep.
4. Live by the 3 E's: energy, enthusiasm and empathy.

5. Watch more movies, play more games and read more books than you did last year.
6. Always pray and make time to exercise.
7. Spend more time with people over the age of 70 and those under the age of six.
8. Dream more while you are awake.
9. Eat more foods that grow on trees and plants, and eat fewer foods that are manufactured in plants or factories.
10. Drink green tea and plenty of water. Eat blueberries, salmon, broccoli, almonds and walnuts.
11. Try to make at least three people smile each day.
12. Clear the clutter from your house, your car and your desk, and let new and flowing energy into your life.
13. Don't waste your precious energy on gossip, energy vampires, issues of the past, negative thoughts or things you cannot control. Instead, invest your energy in the positive, present moment.
14. Realize that life is a school and you are here to learn. Problems are simply part of the curriculum that appear and fade away like algebra class, but the lessons you learn will last a lifetime.
15. Eat breakfast like a king, lunch like a prince and dinner like a college kid with a maxed-out charge card.
16. Life is too short to waste time hating anyone.
17. Don't take yourself so seriously. No one else does.
18. You don't have to win every argument. Agree to disagree.
19. Make peace with your past so it doesn't screw up the present.
20. Don't compare your life to other's. You have no idea what their journeys are all about.
21. Ladies, go on and burn those scented candles, use the 600-thread count sheets, the good china and wear your fancy

lingerie now. Stop waiting for a special occasion. Every day is special.

22. No one is in charge of your happiness except you.
23. Frame every so-called disaster with these words, "In five years, will this matter?"
24. Forgive everyone for everything.
25. What other people think of you is none of your business.
26. Time heals almost everything. Give time, your time!
27. However good or bad a situation is, it will change.
28. Your job won't take care of you when you are sick. Your friends will. Stay in touch with them.
29. Get rid of anything that isn't useful, beautiful or joyful.
30. Envy is a waste of time. You already have all you need.
31. The best is yet to come.
32. No matter how you feel, get up, dress up and show up.
33. Each night before you go to bed, make a list of all you are thankful for.
34. Remember that you are too blessed to be stressed.
35. Enjoy the ride.

These are the things I'd let myself know if I were coming back again, but you can use them now. Regardless of your bank account, age, gender, race or religion, these techniques will bring a sense of balance, abundance and well-being into your life.

Ian Hewitt

THROWING OUT THE TUBE
Ernie Hudson

I graduated from high school, but not the same way or with the same sense of joy and accomplishment that many people share.

My grandmother raised me and I was told to get a high school education, which I did. However, she never said anything about my grades; I graduated with a D average. Then, to make the road to the future even bumpier, I got married at 18. My wife got pregnant right away, and suddenly, one day, it hit me: This was my life. I was working in a factory and I just felt trapped; I had no way out. I thought, "Maybe I'll go to college." But when I tried to get into college, that D average came into play. I couldn't get accepted anywhere.

One night, I just prayed over the whole mess that my life had become. Finally, I drifted off into sleep. I woke up around three in the morning, and I heard a voice saying, "Go downstairs and take the tube out of the TV." You may not believe it, but I did just what I had been told. Of course, when I took the tube out of the TV, my wife thought it was broken. With no TV in the evening, we had to fall back on simple conversation.

For the first time in our married lives, we started to really talk to each other. I found out that my wife was a great reader; she had a deep interest in people and in the world around her, and had the same kind of aspirations that I held in my heart. Well, we just turned our lives around. She was in the ninth grade when we got married; yet she went on to get her Ph.D. I finally got into college at Wayne State, then got a scholarship to Yale, and then I attended the University of Minnesota. On stage or screen, I've been doing what I love to do ever since.

I can never forget that there was one moment when I just *knew* I had to make a change in things. It was a moment of knowing, "I know there's another way, and I'm not seeing it." Sometimes you just have to ask for help. My life has never been—and never will be—the same. I literally woke up.

We watched so much TV those first months we were married; yet I couldn't remember what we watched the night before. Once we started to really communicate with each other, we realized that we both had dreams—a vision of what we wanted to do, and what we wanted to achieve in life. At that moment, we began to climb out of the hole we had gotten ourselves into.

What's your dream? Young people are often told to forget their dreams and prepare for a life of practicality. Acting or any career in theatre, they are told, is impractical. Well, if you really want to act, I say, "Do what you want to do." I talk to people every day who say they want to be an actor, but they only want to be in movies, to be seen on TV, and to be recognized as a celebrity. There is so much more to living a dream.

I discovered acting in college. College is a great place to really understand your craft; to learn what acting is all about. It's not about becoming rich and famous; it's about learning a craft and being able to do for a lifetime. I've been doing it for 40 years, and that's what it's about. To really live the life you love, and to live it with meaning, you may have to change your priorities and your goals. It's not about all the pretended glamour and celebrity, because those things really don't matter at the end of the day.

I have four sons: My two younger boys are in college and my two older sons have graduated from college. They have gotten their advanced degrees. I am so happy for them because they have laid the foundation for living a good life; a decent life. No matter what your career path, the same warning holds true: If you are looking for the glamour, the fame and the recognition, you are searching for an empty treasure chest. You are on the road to a very dead end.

So I would say you should lay out a strong foundation, because that foundation is what is going to carry you over the years. In spite of a few moments of possible glory, you don't really want to end up like so many friends I have known who are angry and bitter and disappointed because they were unfavorably compared to somebody else or they didn't quite get what they thought they wanted.

Reality is this: Find your craft, study, and train. Follow your dream, but never forget: before you can follow a dream, you have to wake up.

Ernie Hudson

GROWING WITH TRUTH
Tildet Varon Schoenbrot

What a blessing it is to live the life I love! I am so grateful to wake up every morning looking forward to another beautiful day, smiling and enthusiastic. I now trust each moment will unfold itself so I can grow, but it was not always this way for me.

I was awakened to this beautiful life by a crisis. All of us have had those moments we call a crisis—disease, divorce, death, separation—not knowing the gateway they will open for us.

I was born in Turkey and studied pharmacy because of my love for healing and understanding the processes of the body. This led me to study complimentary medicine and energy medicine. I moved to the United States at 22, leaving behind everything dear to me for a man who swept me off my feet. I met him on a bus tour in Egypt while he was visiting from the States.

I left my family and friends for him and came to an unknown world. I survived because he became everything to me. We had three beautiful children who are my true blessings and my teachers of life, and I took on the responsibility of making life good for my husband and children. My life was led by their needs and desires, which eventually caused me to lose my identity. My so-called "crisis" knocked on the door to wake me up.

After 20 years of marriage, I was given only one choice: divorce. You can imagine how my world was crushed. I thought my broken pieces would never come together again, but I was wrong. Moments such as this are moments of transformation; they are the moments that open us to a deeper level of wisdom, where answers and solutions begin pouring from within.

My years of studying medicine, energy, healing, spirituality and quantum physics came together like puzzle pieces destined to be linked. The universe had been training me for this moment all along. The so-called "crisis" was, in fact, a wake-up call to reconnect me to my being and push me to express my uniqueness. This transformation moved me to a new consciousness—to a new truth—that led to a new reality.

In this reality, I lived for myself rather than for everyone else. I loved myself unconditionally, even with all of my perceived perfections and imperfections. I began to rekindle my relationship with myself, my values and my desires.

I trusted that people, things and events would come in and out of my life at the perfect time to serve my higher purpose. With that knowledge, I was able to let go of my fears of the future, as well as the guilt and blame of the past.

The feeling of being in and enjoying the present brought empowerment. I wanted every person to live in this reality and bliss. In that spirit, I began a women's healing circle to share my tools. News spread of the knowledge and healing being shared in this group, and more and more people started participating. My life's purpose and gift became clear.

This inspired me to begin my company, Growing With Truth, Inc. This company—through mind, body and soul connection—supports the expansion of mind and heart. Through private sessions, workshops, lectures and study groups, people learn to prosper and to have their lives filled with love, joy and rewards.

I reach many people through my healing circles, classes, lectures, private sessions and meditation CDs, empowering them to live the lives they love. Aligned with their purpose and values, they live from their unique gift of being.

Finding and creating my life's work has brought so much joy, growth, expansion, beauty, love and gratitude to mine and my children's lives. As I serve and empower others, I have become a magnet of abundance. Loving every moment of my life, I know that every person who appears, and every situation that arises, brings a message of love. Now, whether the lesson is perceived as a challenging one or a supporting one, I welcome it with love so that I can learn and continue to grow.

My life reflects my ideals and values, allowing me to express higher qualities of love, well-being, happiness, peace and awareness at a deeper level than I was ever able to in the past. That gift of expression has grown into a unique and beautiful art. I know in my heart that this gift is for each of us. When each one of us is able to express our unique being, it is a winning situation for all of us alike, each contributing his unique gift with love and light to humanity.

I invite you to join me on this journey to explore and connect to the unique gift in all of us. As we connect to the light of our inner being, our life is brightened and guided in a profound way. As our heart leads, our mind follows, breaking the limits it puts on itself. It is our thoughts that create this reality. Let's hold hands in teaching each other how to think. Let's support each other in that thinking. Let's allow each other to live from our beings.

Life is about the meaning we give it. Let's make our lives tell the most amazing stories. In that expression, we can all lead a life that we love, filled with luminosity, love and gratitude.

Tildet Varon Schoenbrot

THREE STEPS TO CLARITY
Alex Mandossian

In my first business venture after college, I lost a quarter of a million dollars. Most of it wasn't mine.

The business was a frozen yogurt and bakery store, and it had turned into a devastating loss. Ninety percent of the money had been handed to me through relatives, grandparents and my parents. I felt a lot of guilt, and I wanted to learn how to prevent it from happening again.

On the drive home from Long Beach, California, I took the long way, and I went to MacArthur Park. I was too embarrassed to go home, so I ended up spending two weeks on a park bench.

I wish I could say it was a brutally cold winter, but it wasn't. It was summer and sunny outside. It was very comfortable. I was sitting right across the street from a hotel owned by one of my father's friends. I figured if it got too uncomfortable, I could at least go up to the hotel and sleep there.

While the bench wasn't too troublesome physically, it wasn't at all fun emotionally. What did I do on the park bench? I thought—a lot—and I learned. I hatched a plan and then I got off that bench and I made things happen.

I wish I could say everything went right after I left the park, but that wasn't the case. It took me five years before I dug myself out of that hole. I never declared bankruptcy but it took me a long time to pay all that money back. After many failed attempts at starting my own business, I eventually got back on my feet in 1994.

But it still wasn't my own business. It was a job on Madison Avenue. And I worked like an animal. There is no other way to look at it. I felt like I was in a galley rowing, like in one of those old movies about Vikings or Romans. I was the chief marketing officer of a company on Madison Avenue, and I worked 16-hour days. Why? Not only did I want to keep my job, but I also wanted to make more money. The only way I could do that was to get a promotion.

I didn't get a pay raise every month as I do now, and I had very little freedom. In fact, if I continued to work at that place, I would probably have lost my marriage and would not have had the two beautiful kids I have today.

I had my children late in life because of that job. I almost lost my marriage because of that job. And I stayed at that job until 2000.

So, how did I make the leap from working stiff to entrepreneur who takes time off to enjoy my family? I did it with the help of these three secrets.

Secret Number 1: Create Your Master To-Do List.
Each morning you should come to your clean desk with your completed master to-do list. That way, you can start your day by attacking the list and crossing things out. Isn't that a lot easier than trying to invent things to do? Don't write more than 20 actions per day. And when you prioritize your to-do list, make sure you put the fun first. That will put you on a positive note for the rest of the day. At the end of the day, if you have any actions left, make sure you put them on the page for tomorrow. Then crumple up and throw the old sheet away. It's done.

Secret Number 2: Block Out Your Daily Prime-Time Hours.
What is a prime-time hour? A prime-time hour is anything you control 100 percent and is going to generate revenue for you now or sometime in the future. I have four prime-time hours a day. You should have at least one or two. Think about it. If you only have one prime-time hour a day and you work five days a week—many of us work many more than that—that's 225 work days per year. At one hour a day, you're giving yourself 225 prime-time revenue-generating hours a year. Don't you think you can generate some revenue with that? I think so. You'd be robbing yourself if you didn't. I encourage you to block out one prime-time hour a day starting next week.

Which hour is the most important of the day? The first hour. Why? You are more fresh in the morning than you are after having been beaten down by the day's events. You start with the positive.

But, what is the first thing you typically do when you get in front of your computer? Check e-mail. Is that an interruption? Yes. And worse, it can start your whole day off badly. What if you wake up and see an e-mail from someone asking for a refund? Doesn't that put you into some type of emotional tailspin?

Now, what if you do this instead: Rather than checking your e-mail, generate revenue for one full hour first. Don't you feel good about yourself? You've already crossed out some things on your master action to-do list. You can handle that bad news a little better now. See what I am saying?

When people get the bad news first, they concentrate on that bad news and not the good news. So, start with good news.

Always avoid the daily interruptions you can control during your prime-time hours. That means no e-mail, no voice mail, no phone calls, no letters. Tell your family it's prime-time and have them support you (unless it's an emergency).

Start with a revenue-generating activity, and you will feel great about yourself.

Secret Number 3: During Prime-Time, Put Pressure on Yourself by Using a Timer.
I put pressure on myself. Since I can't manage time, I manage actions. I have a nine-dollar timer that measures up to 60 minutes. I recommend you set your timers to 50 or 55 minutes. I set mine to 47 minutes. Why? I like to have a 13-minute break. I am greedy with my time off. However, when I started, I set it for 55 minutes and gave myself a 5-minute break. I suggest you do the same. Put the timer where you can see it, right next to your computer screen. When that thing is counting down, is that putting pressure on you or what? When the beeper goes off, stop everything you're doing. It's incredibly important because you've got to give yourself a break.

These tips allow you to get more done, faster, better and with less effort. If you practice them daily, you'll be astonished at how much more efficient you are and how much more you're able to get done in a day. The path to success will be much clearer, and the question, "What should I do now?" will have an obvious answer.

Alex Mandossian

I'VE GOT THE POWER
Michal Yahalomi Noah, C.H.T.

"What the mind can conceive and believe, the mind of men can achieve."—Napoleon Hill

I was married at the age of 18 and became a mother at the age of 20. As you can imagine, I had many struggles. I lived in rented apartments which I lost every few months. Things eventually got to the point that we could not take it anymore and we decided to leave Israel and move to America. My firstborn was eight years old at the time. We made the move with nothing but hope in our hearts, having no money or education and knowing very little English. It seemed that everything was against us in those days.

My husband and I worked hard jobs simply to survive. I recall all those years being filled with negative thoughts and feelings. My attitude toward myself and my life was truly destructive. I was constantly judging and criticizing myself. I welcomed all negative thoughts, felt sorry for myself and hated my life. I blamed all my problems on myself and filled my head with comments like "I am not smart enough" or "I don't have enough education."

My head was packed with all kinds of disempowering self-talk. You can imagine how I felt while entertaining these kinds of thoughts. This was a cycle I thought I had no control of. About five years went by with these destructive thoughts in my mind.

During this period, I went through an experience that completely changed my understanding of reality. What I am about to share with you was an eye-opening experience. I was given an opportunity to experience a hypnotic, guided-imagery journey to the time of my baby's delivery. I didn't understand then what it meant, but I agreed to participate out of curiosity. I was sitting down when I was asked in a very gentle, low voice to sit back, relax and close my eyes. I followed the voice and its instruction. I was led through a progressive relaxation process that required relaxing every muscle in my body. When I was deeply relaxed, I was asked to picture a mental screen in my mind's eye. I was told on that screen I could project images of my future baby's delivery.

In my mind's eye I saw myself at the event of my baby's delivery entering a room. I was able to see the delivery room in vivid detail. I could hear and see my husband and the doctors coming in and out of the room. I saw a nurse and noticed exactly how she looked. When the delivery began, I saw, heard and felt everything I perceived on my mental screen.

The baby came out and didn't make a sound. For a long while, with my eyes closed, I started to cry and feared something might be wrong. The hypnotist asked me to take a deep, slow breath and relax even more, suggesting that I could create a new, more desirable picture. So I did. Then, I could see myself and my baby surrounded by a healing golden light. It truly felt magical. The baby was fine, and yes, he did cry. Everything was okay and I was guided out of the hypnotic state. I opened my eyes, felt very relaxed and just smiled. Later that week I gave this experience only minor significance.

The day of actual delivery finally came and we headed to the hospital. I was led to my delivery room and as soon as I walked in I was amazed to realize it was the same room I had seen. Everything looked the way I perceived it, including the furniture, pictures and colors. I remember smiling when the nurse walked in and I felt certainty knowing it was the nurse I had seen in my vision. I had never physically seen her before. I now felt confident and in control.

I realized that I was now living and experiencing physically what I had perceived mentally. You see, I already knew how this was going to end. The experience altered my life completely. Being curious, I started to explore, looking for answers and that led me to read many books which dealt with the mind and how to use its unlimited powers. I listened to CDs, watched DVDs, took courses and attended seminars. I loved all that I found. I began to understand that I had great power within me and that all I needed to do was acknowledge and learn to use it. I understood that I was responsible for my life, and made a decision to take control of my thought patterns—and so can you!

Now, take a moment to stop and think about your current life and about your desired future. What kind of experiences would you like to have? I am sure you want the very best for yourself. You surely want a bright, joyful, fulfilling life. Well, if you think you can, I believe you can. Be aware of your thought patterns. Create the habit of entertaining empowering thoughts. The conversations you have in your mind about yourself have a tremendous impact on who you become and what you experience.

What are the things you say to yourself over and over again? You must understand that negative self-talk is very damaging to your self-esteem and self-confidence, which prevents you from performing your very best. You begin to believe the things you say about yourself. Decide to improve your inner dialogue.

So listen, pay attention to your self-talk and start replacing the negative with positive. Thoughts are things—believe that to be the case. You are what you think you are and you create your own world and reality with your thoughts. You have the power, by thinking constructive thoughts, to create pleasant feelings and emotions. As you think, so you feel, and the way you feel will have a great impact on the way you behave and what you do. This determines the outcome. Pay close attention to your emotions, as you can learn from them. They send signals to you notifying you that there is something you need to learn to change and act upon. When feeling negative emotions, it simply means you should check your thoughts or beliefs or some meaning you give to a certain past experience.

So choose to feel great now. Just start focusing your mind on what empowers, inspires and motivates you. The use of words is also very important. Using certain words causes you to feel a certain way. The words you are using can have a great impact on yourself and others and what you experience in your life. Start to use affirmations. When you do this with strong emotions and repeat the affirmation over and over again, you eventually start to believe in them.

Here is a simple yet powerful exercise for you to do daily: Decide to put aside five to 10 minutes of your time and make sure to not be disturbed. Sit back comfortably in a quiet place. Close your eyes and take a deep, slow breath. Hold it in for about three seconds and exhale slowly, simply letting go of all the tension in your body. Allow yourself to relax. Do it several times until you become deeply calm and relaxed, physically and mentally. Now imagine that you have a mental screen (with your eyes still closed) and on that screen you can create and project the images of your desired outcome. Ask yourself, "Who do I want to be? What do I want to have and achieve?" Use your senses to create a clear picture of the ideal you. See the sights, hear the sounds and feel the feelings and make it as real as you can. Notice what you see and hear. How do you feel? Make the images as vivid as possible and hold on to the pleasant feelings they create in you." While you do that, reinforce it with affirmations such as, "I am happy," "I am relaxed," and "I am confident." Whatever quality you desire, affirm for yourself. Hear, see and feel yourself as already being that person and having that quality. When you are done, simply open your eyes and sit down and create a plan of small things you can do each day to fulfill your heart's desire. Immediately take action, based on your plan. Do that daily and miracles will start happening in your life. Love and accept yourself and no matter what, always smile! Know and remember that you conduct your own life. It is your birthright to live a harmonious life, so claim it now! Only you can create the life you want to lead and you already have all you need to create the life you want within, so take charge!

You can reshape, redesign and rewrite your life script. Make it a beautiful one. Believe in yourself. Think, talk, feel and act in a new and great way. You deserve to be happy, healthy and abundant in every aspect of your life. Access the power that lies within you. Lead your life with excitement. Your journey has now begun.

Michal Yahalomi Noah, C.H.T.

FORBIDDEN TO EXCEL
Charlinda Wilkinson

I was born and raised in a small town in Ontario, Canada in the '50s and '60s. That in itself should be considered a success, but does anyone actually think or feel that way? I have never heard anyone suggest this, not even the counselors I have gone to to help eliminate my own self-motivated system failure button. Maybe the reason I acquired the thought process of believing I was a failure is because I started out in life thinking that I could do anything as a male. Let me explain that statement: I was a tomboy until I got stuck with boobs. What an awakening *that* was! All of a sudden, people started treating me differently. Boy, was I confused!

I thought that I could play sports aggressively (and I *was* aggressive), as long as I wanted to. I played fair and I played well. When I look back now, I realize that, even then, I had to be twice as good as the guys I was playing with and against in order to be accepted. I was highly competitive, but as a woman, I was not supposed to be.

All of a sudden, my life was run by a different set of rules and I didn't own the guidebook. As a woman, you are not supposed to want to succeed outside the home. Be a good wife, then mother and then you're finished! Well, if that was how things were, I would do my best to work with it.

I did what was expected of me. I got married at 18, got pregnant and had a baby. Now what? I was very dissatisfied with my life, so I had another child. During my younger years, I had been very active and fit, but now I was not. As a mature woman—a mother— it was no longer acceptable to be active. Unfortunately, my aggressive nature didn't want to be downplayed or ignored. Maybe I could stay active by taking exercise classes. Subconsciously, I guess I wanted some kind of exercise that would help me calm my aggressive nature, so I started yoga. It was my savior in many ways.

My mother was a stay-at-home mom, as was my mother-in-law. They were my only examples. Don't get me wrong, there is nothing wrong with being a stay-at-home-mom if that is your desire, but I thought that was my only option.

I look back now and see the many successes in my life, but at the time I was living them, I didn't see them as successful. During my yoga classes, I was blessed with an instructor who saw great teaching potential in me. She encouraged me to get qualified to teach yoga. This was acceptable because it didn't really earn me a lot of money, and it didn't take a lot of time away from being a "proper" wife and mother.

My next success was teaching exercise classes—not just yoga. As I was teaching these classes, the local recreation director encouraged me to take the college course to become certified. If my husband had not told me at this juncture that I was not "allowed" to take the class, I probably would have just let it go—accepted the encouragement as a compliment and left it at that. In a way, I guess, I should thank my husband for "forbidding" me to expand myself because it started me on my present course of learning. Off to college I went, where I worked for and earned my diploma.

What a surprise to find out that I was an intelligent, interesting and driven woman! This realization was the beginning of the end of my marriage. I was no longer willing to accept the limitations forced upon me.

My next step was to become fit and active again, so why not umpire baseball as well as play it? I certified and umpired for more than five years. It was not "normal" to even want to be an umpire, let alone a female umpire.

At this time, I also became a writer for the local newspaper. The *Pembroke Advertiser News* wanted contributions from its readers. They were interested in columns that would be of interest while imparting knowledge. For a year, I wrote about yoga, exercise and the reasons why we need to do these activities.

My next success was initiation into television. A woman in the exercise classes I taught thought that I would be a good inspiration to others. Me? Why would anyone be interested in watching me on TV? The woman worked at the local cable station and they were looking for new and different shows to air. She became my director and talked me into it by telling me that I did not have to watch what I had done if I didn't want to, and I didn't for over a year. When I finally had the courage to watch what other people were telling me was "good stuff," I wanted to learn more. I became the writer and producer of a show called *Forever Alive*. I starred in, wrote and produced the show for two years.

My next project was a news show for the Canadian Armed Forces called *CFB Awareness*. This show was the best project I had done in my life. I realized that I had something to say and people were listening and enjoying it. My director and I won an award for the show and, because I had to have certain political clearance qualifications, my horizons expanded yet again.

I had lived in this small town for many years and the most difficult thing I had to deal with was that everyone knew who I was and where I had come from. That is to say, that as an "army brat" and a woman, I could go no further. It is so difficult to fight this thinking on a daily basis. I felt that if I didn't get out of there, I might as well accept what I was "supposed to be" and live with it! I don't think so! On top of that, I was a divorcee with two children to support with little help from their father.

I did get out of Ontario, although it took me a year to find the courage and get organized to move. I sold what I did not need, stored what I could and packed my car to leave for Calgary, Alberta. I did not know anyone there, nor did I have a job lined up.

What a shock to find out when I got here that the 13 years of qualifications, training and certificates I had achieved in Ontario were not acknowledged in Alberta! I would have to get recertified, but I didn't have the money to do that. Now what? Once again, people were telling me that I was not "good enough." I suppose I could have just quit and gone home, as my parents were encouraging me to do.

I knew that I needed more education, so I went to college for a marketing diploma. This course got me organized and changed my thinking from, "Everything I try to do I fail," to helping me to recognize my strengths and success. To make my success story even better, here I am today, with many successes behind me and still going strong. Only you can put the roadblocks up for yourself.

Charlinda Wilkinson

OH, OLIVER! (FROM THE WAKE UP LIVE MOVIE)
Liz Vassey

I was a very, very, very shy kid, when I was three or four. I just did-n't talk to strangers and I was very uncomfortable in front of groups.

I started acting when I was nine, and I started in theater—actually musical theater. It was then that I saw my sister in a play, and I went to my mom, and I said, "I think I would really like to try that." She said, "Oh, I think that would be great. I'm not taking you. Your sister can take you out. I don't want any part of seeing you get up on that stage and seeing what happens."

The first play I auditioned for was *Oliver* and I sang for it, and I played Oliver. I remember getting up on that stage and actually feeling very much at home for the first time.

Once you've had that moment, I would say you have to be incredibly persistent. Do not believe too much of the good or of the bad. Stay true to yourself because they are trying to change you and fix you and mold you. I think what's different or peculiar about you is what's special about you in the first place. Don't lose it.

Liz Vassey

DISCOVER YOUR TRUE POWER
Peter Field

It was not until I was 47 that I understood the enormous power that lies dormant within each of us, just waiting to be discovered and unleashed upon the world.

I entered the corporate world at 16, and although I enjoyed what many would consider a "successful" career, something was missing. The executive titles and material rewards did not provide the fulfilment and excitement they promised. Instead, each step up the corporate ladder increased my to-do list and decreased precious time with family and friends. I felt trapped by the expectations of others rather than being authentic to myself.

It took me 30 years to find the courage to leave the corporate world and everything I had worked hard to attain so that I could pursue my passion for personal development. It was very challenging. I strongly believed in the comfort and security of a full-time job, and yet here I was at the age of 47, self-employed for the first time. I had no client base, no network and no guarantee of future income. It was a leap of faith and required me to embrace a new belief: You can earn a living doing what you love.

Replacing decades of thinking is painful and scary and can be slow without expert help. So I made the decision early on to do whatever it took to learn from those who maintained the lifestyle I desired. As a result, I traveled the globe to be mentored by successful entrepreneurs who live and follow their passions daily. Although my journey continues, the insights and awareness I have developed over the last few years have been life-changing and I am now on a mission to help people understand that it is never too late to wake up and live the life you love.

My book, *Lighten Your Load,* is dedicated to this cause. It has received favorable acclaim from teachers from the hit movie *The Secret* and has been written to help people discover just how powerful and magnificent they really are.

We have been conditioned to believe our power is derived from things outside of ourselves. It's in the job title, the amount of money in the bank or the amount of our material possessions. But these are *effects,* and as with all *effects* in the external world, they can be lost as easily as they are won.

The real power lies in understanding the *cause* of everything you wish to experience in your life, and to do this, you have to let go of some deeply held, erroneous beliefs.

The first belief is that what we see, hear, taste, touch and smell is reality, and if we can't perceive it with our senses, it doesn't exist. Nothing is further from the truth. Our senses enable us to connect and interact with our outer world, but they do not reflect true reality. Even as you are reading this book, electromagnetic forces such as electricity, radio waves and cellular phone signals are all around you. Even though you cannot see them, you know they are there. Similar limitations apply to our other senses. This is important because it means—on a practical basis—you do not have to tangibly see all the resources you need in order to achieve your big goals and dreams. There are invisible resources you can access which are far more powerful than the resources you can see.

The second belief is that life "happens" to you and you are powerless to change your current circumstance. In addition to the five physical senses which enable you to connect and interact with your outer world, you have also been gifted with six intellectual factors: reason, will, imagination, perception, intuition and memory. These enable you to connect and interact with your inner—or mental—world. Most people don't know they have these factors and fewer still use them on a daily basis. Yet, it is only through their proper use that you can access your true power.

In the same way that every building begins as a picture in the mind of the architect, everything you wish to create begins as a picture on the screen of your mind. You can use your imagination to picture things that already exist—such as your favorite luxury car or house—as well as things that don't yet exist—such as the creation of a new business or the launch of an exciting new idea. By using another factor—your will— you can focus your attention on this picture to the exclusion of all other information craving your attention. As this picture of what you want is held on the screen of your mind, it is impressed upon your subconscious and becomes your dominant vibration. This vibration—more commonly referred to as feeling—expresses itself through behaviors and actions to produce your desired results.

The problem is that we have been conditioned to focus on what we don't want, such as debt or poor health, and we let these thoughts—normally associated with powerful emotion—dictate the picture we hold in our conscious mind. The pictures of what we don't want are similarly impressed upon our subconscious mind and expressed through our body in behaviors and actions to produce more of the unwanted results. In addition, the pictures and thoughts of what we don't want set in motion a magnetic force to attract into our lives everything that is in vibrational harmony with them. Thus, through the Law of Attraction, we unwittingly draw into our lives people, circumstances and events that are in vibrational resonance with the thoughts and feelings we have about what we don't want. This is why so many people find it difficult to get out of debt or overcome illness and feel powerless to change it. Why? Because we are conditioned to believe that we can get what we want by resisting what we don't want, but that is not how the universe works. We live in a universe based on attraction and there is no such thing as exclusion. When we look at something we do not want and shout, "No!" to it, we are not pushing it away—we are drawing it to us.

So, what is the answer? The answer lies in understanding the power you have to change the picture through the wonderful gift of your imagination. Turn away from sight—what you see with your physical eyes—and start operating from *vision*. In my imagination, *Lighten Your Load* was published with celebrity endorsements before the opening words were written. This power is also within you right now, patiently waiting to be discovered. So reclaim your power today. Use your powerful imagination to build a detailed picture of exactly how you want your life to be, and when you impress this picture upon your subconscious mind, invisible forces will delight and amaze you with their support. Inspiration, creative solutions, people, circumstances and events will appear as if by magic and you will come to know, perhaps for the first time, that you really *can* live the life you love!

Peter Field

THE SQUARE BUBBLE
Geoff Akins

"Geoff is a modern-day Johnny Appleseed, spreading his message far and wide, only working with bubbles instead of apple seed, and children's souls instead of earth."—Dr. Tom Howard

During my first year working in special education, I had an amazing experience with a young boy who was autistic. My heart went out to him because he never interacted with any of the teachers or students.

One day, for my own amusement, I blew bubbles in class. The boy stopped what he was immersed in and came over. He sat down in front of me and actually made eye contact for the first and only time that entire school year. This was huge! I didn't know what to do, so I just kept blowing bubbles for as long as he remained engaged, grateful for this brief connection. I wondered what else I could do with the bubbles that might hold his attention for a longer period of time.

This interaction was the seed of an idea that eventually grew into what I now call the "Bubble Wonder Show." It's a magical, motivational show that uses the art and science of "bubbleology." During my performance I demonstrate a variety of bubble tricks, such as making caterpillars, volcanoes, ice cream cones and merry-go-rounds.

The theme of the show is "Anything is possible!" To prove this truth, I share with the students my dream to create something impossible: a square bubble. I always do it by the end of the show. I intentionally fail a few times along the way in order to model persistence and to teach that just because something is possible doesn't mean it's always going to be easy. If you have a goal and a dream in your heart, you can't give up when it becomes difficult.

Right around this same time, I was awarded a full scholarship for a master's in special education. I was excited by my good fortune, but when it came time to sign on the dotted line I suffered a full-blown panic attack. I couldn't breathe or swallow, my heart was pounding in my chest, and I was sweating and shivering at the same time.

In the end, I turned down the scholarship. My family, friends and colleagues didn't understand, but I had to trust my intuition. In the back of my mind, I wondered, "Do I have what it takes to make it as a full-time performer?" I was so full of doubt and fear that I just avoided the decision altogether. If my friends and family thought I was crazy to pass up a free scholarship, what would they think of my leaving a secure job with health insurance to pursue a dream of playing with bubbles for a living?

Word of my skills as a motivational speaker and bubbleologist continued to spread. The new school year started at the end of August, and by October I had already used all of my vacation days, personal days and sick days to perform for other schools, daycare centers and libraries. I had reached a crossroads and had to make a decision. Should I stay, or should I go?

The truth is I was ready for a change as I realized how little of my real gifts and talents were being used in my current position. That year I was assigned to a severely mentally and physically handicapped teenaged student named Jaeden. Confined to a wheelchair and unable to walk or talk, Jaeden was as helpless as a baby. I had to dress him, feed him and help him to the toilet. These additional responsibilities were new to me, and I was way out of my comfort zone. I prayed for guidance.

One day our class went to see the movie *The Polar Express*. I muscled Jaeden's wheelchair into an empty space and settled into a seat next to him to watch the film. The heart of the story is how the young hero is unable to hear the sound of a sleigh bell (a symbol of the true spirit of Christmas) because he has lost his faith. In his innocence, he convinces himself to believe and rekindles his hope by repeating over and over, "I believe, I believe, I believe." When he finally overcomes his doubt and rings the bell again, he hears its joyous sound at last!

When that bell rang out, I experienced an epiphany. I suddenly realized the missing piece in my own situation. It was at once both simple and profound. I had to *believe*! I closed my eyes and silently affirmed with absolute certainty, "I believe I can make a living doing what I truly love. I believe God will help guide me in this process. I believe!"

At that precise moment in that darkened theatre, Jaeden reached over from his wheelchair and held my hand. My heart soared at his divinely-timed touch. You see, for Jaeden to initiate contact was amazing enough, but to reach over and gently take my hand into his at that exact moment was nothing short of miraculous! This was the sign I so desperately needed. It was humbling how empowered I became by the most powerless person I knew.

In that moment, I knew everything would work out just fine—and it has! Soon after my cosmic wake-up call, I was hired to perform my "Bubble Wonder Show" for three weeks at the Bloomfield Museum in Jerusalem; a week of shows in Hong Kong and southern China followed.

When I finally returned home again, I resigned from my "real job" and started my own company: The Art of Wonder, LLC. I now earn a six-figure income living a life I love. I've worked for the National Geographic Channel, appeared on national television, and I have been hired to perform during the 2008 Summer Olympics in China!

I travel all over the country, planting seeds of possibility by empowering children and young-at-heart adults to follow their dreams, no matter how impossible they might seem. I show by example how "anything is possible" by creating square bubbles and by sharing the story of my own journey from self-doubt to belief.

So now, dear reader, I reach out, take your hand and ask:

"What is your impossible dream? What is it you truly want to do? What is *your* square bubble?"

Just remember William Arthur Ward's quote: If you believe it, you can achieve it!

Geoff Akins

FREEDOM
Dr. Michael Beckwith

I free myself from the need to judge any person, nation or event. My consciousness is at peace, for it is now rooted and grounded in the Spirit. My thinking is premised on Infinite Mind, and I am established in love, compassion and forgiveness.

From the center of my heart, I radiate compassion to all beings, knowing that their pain is bathed in the Infinite Love of the Spirit.

I awaken the spirit of forgiveness within me. Even now it fills my consciousness with loving kindness toward myself with all beings. I judge not, lest I be judged. I love with the unconditional love of God.

Right here, right now, Divine Love loves through me. Divine Right Action frees me from the errors of human judgment and causes me to know that all beings are emanations of the One Life.

The true spiritual essence is all I know of each person. I think rightly, and I love greatly. I live to let love express itself through me.

I accept the fullness of life and am a distribution center of compassion, forgiveness, and love. I am blessed and prospered by Divine Love as it flows through me now.

I declare my faith in God and release material patterns of behavior. I know that God is at the center of life and I depend upon that which projected all creation as its own to be the source of eternal safety and security for all beings.

Dr. Michael Beckwith

ALL YOU NEED IS LOVE
Rizo Santos Saverio

The rhythm of the ocean and the waves crashing upon the shore brought me back to the present with both fear and hope: Fear of love and hope for love.

In the late afternoon at the beach, long shadows moved around me, their unclear borders in stark contrast with the sharp edges of my mind.

"All You Need is Love" had been my anthem through the time my husband and I met, married and put our children through school. We had more than 30 years together, then nothing. I saw my life's anthem change from "All You Need is Love" to some version of a bad country song, "If You Need Love, Don't Bother Asking for It."

My heart was always in the right place. However, early life never prepared me to effectively deal with the differences and problems that might arise in marriage or elsewhere. Somehow, things were supposed to just work out when intentions were good.

Decades were lost while trying to find the script for our lives, and my best efforts fell short each time. Nothing I tried ever measured up and tracks that were left embedded in my soul made the changes almost more painful than I could bear.

Some problems were present when my husband and I met. Others we managed to develop and nourish together. I felt overwhelmed by their number, size and complexity. Working on the assumption that love would somehow clear the path one day only made me more vulnerable. The more love I poured out, the less it seemed to matter.

After much confusion, I came to the conclusion that love was hardly what we needed—at least not the kind of love that makes you deny your feelings or that makes you lay low, hoping to survive just one more day. Love was too complicated.

Different types of ideal love were very different in reality; they seem somewhat intangible, differing according to our needs and back-ground. Perhaps the mores of society expect sacrifice to the love given by women, and self-fulfillment and entitlement to the love men expect to receive. Overall, love seems to be that which we lack in ourselves and expect to see in the object of our love.

I believed my missing half was out there, and collected heartbreaks when reality closed door after door opened in vain. Much pain accu-mulated while I searched for that all-consuming feeling to complete myself—the day I would become whole. For decades, I looked at my partner and myself as pieces of an incomplete puzzle. This feeling was so strong that it kept me from moving onto a higher spiritual plane. It was a requirement that no other human could satisfy. No one could complete what I felt was missing.

Riding on the swooshing and crashing waves, my mind started to frame a clear picture of what I needed to change. Days like that— glorious and indescribable in their hues—would likely come and go as they had for millennia. When I saw myself and the days of my life on that beach, I had to admit my life was likely to come to an end much sooner. Death, at that moment, seemed palpable. Already, stormy nights had alternated with the glorious days of light; cold and warmth, hunger and satisfaction, need and appreciation.

Those shadows extending, dancing forth and yonder, gave anchor to the thought that my life could also be borderless, heading to a natural, but rather inglorious, sunset I was not yet ready to embrace.

I stood and decided to live as I had before my life was shattered. No, not like before. Better!

Why repeat what I already knew? Off to uncharted waters, unbound by the fears on the path of achieving my potential. No fading into shadows without promise of dawn. That was my wake-up moment!

Parallels existed between what I still wanted to do in life and the chance to use my gifts, along with the limits given by time and energy, which seemed the same as the limits of each day. Only when you can say you touched at least part of the skies should you allow yourself to reflect the shadows, inclining gently into the slumber of night.

The time came to take inventory of what lay before me—the raw material available to stir my spirit into a new expression of its form. Looking back, I could see my whole life had been a preperation for that moment. My love of reading, observing, comparing and researching gave me the foundation for a good start. Tentatively, I could imagine myself a blossom after the rain, cleansed of old, erroneous thoughts. I gained new perspective about why I had abandoned my dreams. It had been difficult to absorb a different society, restricting myself for the sake of raising a family the way I thought right. The flame that gave the younger me so much light and life was near extinction from so much effort to find sense in everyday life.

Long after discarding "All You Need is Love" as a cruel joke of commercialism, I returned to the realization of its truth: "Love is all you need." *Love* is what we are. It is present. Always.

Now, when I walk down the street and catch my reflection in a mirror, I recognize how I'd always had it with me, how it had tried to show me its face. When I look into the eyes of others, even those of strangers, I am comfortable with what I get back. I now understand that the love of my life will reflect to me exactly what I feel. We are a part of the infinite and eternal energy that holds together each and every thought, image and action in the universe. In our short stay in this stage of learning, we are really anxious to return to our wholeness as spirits. Everything takes a second seat when we awaken to the magnitude of our potential. We are part of a great experiment to learn the way back to eternal love energy.

I feel more secure each day; I will never suffer as I did before. It is amazing to me that it took so long for me to understand such a simple and rewarding blessing. When I struggle now, it is to move past the forces keeping me ignorant of the paths to overcoming doubt, need and fear. Before my wake-up moment, I constantly worried about finding and keeping love. Now I see how pointless that is.

Wherever I go, I am complete and whole. Love makes me happy to be me and I am looking forward to sample all that is open before me. This restlessness that remains is part of our spirits' desire to reconnect, to return to our source.

We are all little swatches of the fabric of the universe, both a reflection and a part of its mystery.

As we cross paths with other souls that complete the energy field we came from, in their eyes we see ourselves—as they also see themselves in us—the perfect love we always wanted to have and to hold.

In our wake-up moments, may we together realize how perfect we are and how we can be present for others on the way to finding perfect love, which is all we need.

May blessings fill our hearts forever.

Rizo Santos Saverio

ABIE'S STORY
Dr. Rashid A. Buttar

My son, Abie, lost his ability to speak when he was about 14 months old. His limited vocabulary of about 15 words rapidly disappeared within a few weeks of his third set of inoculations. His first word, "Abu" (meaning "father"), was the first to disappear.

Abie was born January 25, 1999. Ten months prior to his birth—one month before his conception—I decided I would no longer see autistic patients. My name in Arabic means "one who stays on the right path." Well, I wasn't living up to my name. God had destined for me to do something else than what I thought, and this was, at least in retrospect, nothing more than His upping the ante, saying, "You're going to do what I tell you to do!"

We had decided not to inoculate Abie due to the presence of thimerosol (ethyl mercury), which is still used as a preservative in vaccinations. I am considered one of the leading authorities in metal toxicology and there was no way I would let my son be exposed to mercury, the second most toxic substance known to man. However, unbeknownst to me, my former wife had gotten him the regularly scheduled vaccines. By the age of two, he was "developmentally delayed."

It was obvious the loss of speech was more than a little transient delay in Abie's development. As time passed, the pediatricians kept saying the same thing, "There's probably nothing here, so just wait. Maybe he's a late developer." I knew there was something wrong. It wasn't that he never acquired the ability to speak. He lost it! A 12- to 15-word vocabulary isn't significant, but it's still a dozen words, and they were all gone.

I didn't know what to do. Although I had treated hundreds of patients with mercury and lead toxicity, I had never treated a child this young. I knew from treating autistic children in the past that his behavior was the same and that terrified me. I knew my son was not supposed to be in this state.

I spent thousands of hours over the next few years, many hours late at night, studying, researching, learning, crying and praying my son would be returned to normal. I pleaded, begged and threatened God. I bartered with the Creator, negotiating my arms or my legs in exchange for the return of my son. But throughout this ordeal, Abie always looked at me with eyes that said, "Don't worry, Dad. I know you'll figure it out."

Of course, the rest of the story is now a matter of public record and history, but for those who don't know, Abie's fourth set of tests showed mercury. As a result, I developed an innovative method to treat him, which up until that time had never been contemplated. Five months after I initiated the new treatment, Abie went from not speaking to possessing a vocabulary of more than 500 words, and he ended up becoming the youngest formal witness to appear and testify before the U.S. Congress.

Today, people ask me if he's "normal." He's anything but normal. He's exceptionally handsome, gentle, ahead of his peers academically and athletically, and a Triple Crown Black Belt state champion in Tae Kwon Do at age eight and now ranked "Top 10 in the World" in forms and sparring at age ten. He touches everyone who meets him, and to know him is to truly love him. The efficacy of Abie's treatment is now well documented. We have treated nearly 700 children from all over the world, and many doctors on five continents have reproduced our results with tremendous success when following our protocol.

It is now painfully obvious I was deviating from my destiny, and in retrospect, it's pretty clear Abie is here for a specific reason. His name (Abid) in Arabic actually means "one who serves God," and I believe he's already fulfilled that mission. The DVD titled *Autism, The Misdiagnosis of Our Future Generations* tells the full story and discloses the truth about autism.

The Difference Between Success and Failure

So why am I telling this story? It's because of one thing that I believe is essential for every human being to know in order to truly empower themselves. It's the crucial defining factor dictating ultimate success versus certain defeat. It is why Abie is completely healthy and normal today (as normal as a gifted child can be).

First, no matter what your situation, remember: It could always be worse. You may think these are motivational words, but they are meant to be a slap in the face to wake you up to reality. No matter how bad you think your situation is, it is nothing compared to what some people endure on a daily basis. Look at the poverty in South Africa, the hunger in Ethiopia, the atrocities beyond our comprehension committed in other parts of the world.

Now, if I said you could break through absolutely any barrier, any self-constraint and any issue, would you believe me? If I told you this information is supported by several Nobel Prize laureates and is embedded so deeply in quantum physics that it would be impossible for any intelligent person to refute this information, would you believe me?

Herein lies the key. Whatever you believe you can or cannot do, you are correct. It all comes down to belief. If you believe what I have said, it will be as I have said, just as my life was changed when I believed Abie would be returned to me. If, however, you believe what you just read is hype, then guess what, my friend: It won't even amount to that much.

This is true whether you are facing cancer or dealing with financial issues, athletic events or personal relationships. But the belief must be complete, total and without a doubt. It must burn inside you to the point that no other option is possible. You must believe 100 percent. Whatever the desire is, you must completely believe it to be the only possible outcome.

Basis of Choice

Make sure your heart is open and that you have no preconceived notions. Whatever your intuition tells you, that will be the correct answer for you. My hope is for everyone to learn, understand, fully embrace and experience the power of this because it is the essence of all achievement—physically, financially, spiritually and emotionally.

I wish each of you great fortune and success. Remember, everything you will ever face in life will always boil down to one word, and that word is simply "*choice*." It is your God-given right to be able to make a choice in anything and everything you do. All choices have a root that can be distilled in one of two possible sources: love or fear. One is real, the other is an illusion. The question you have to ask yourself now is which root is the basis of the choices you will make. It's your move. Make it a good one.

Dr. Rashid A. Buttar

WE ARE EXACTLY WHERE WE CHOOSE TO BE
Gregory Scott Reid

Before you get your hair in a bunch from the title, let me begin by stating that I fully understand there are unique outside influences that affect our lives from time to time. On the same note, it is also understood that, for the most part, we—ourselves—have chosen to be precisely where we are today.

Have you ever noticed that the same people who complain about their jobs, relationships, and situations are the exact same ones who put themselves in that position in the first place? Let's face facts. If you don't like your job or current relationship, change it!

If it's your job you dislike...
Understand that you are the one who circled the ad in the paper or went down to the office and filled out your application.

If it's a relationship that needs some adjustment...
Please accept that you are the one who courted the person you are in a relationship with. You are the one who asked the person out and acted on your best behavior.

In other words, you chose your situation. The good news here is that just as soon as you realize this, you can move forward to adjust your circumstances accordingly. You hold the power for change!

This can be done by asking for a new job within the organization, going to school to get a degree toward the field you desire, or even making that conscious decision to leave your current relationship.

The bottom line is that you have the ability to choose the life you live.

A great friend and mentor, John Assaraf, once said, "Life is a professional sport, not an amateur one. Play it like a professional and you will get the results a professional gets, play it like an amateur and the results go the other way."

Let me pose a question that you've read on coffee mugs and t-shirts for years: What would you do if you knew you could not fail?

Never has there been a soul who claimed on his deathbed that he wished more time had been spent in the office. We are in a wonderful age of opportunity. Life truly is what we make of it. From another viewpoint, look at it this way: Why did our forefathers give their lives for us? Did they suffer the ultimate price so that we could wallow in discomfort? Did they offer us the chance for personal freedom? They gave us the ability to choose our own destiny and make the most out of every breath God gives us.

I pose a challenge. Make a list of situations you wish could be different. Then have the courage and conviction to take responsibility for your part. The final task is to take action toward building a brighter tomorrow. After all, we are exactly where we choose to be!

Gregory Scott Reid

SEIZE THE DAY
Pam Robertson, Ph.D.

Powerful changes bring about powerful change.

Things had been spinning around me for awhile, but everything got really heated one slippery January day when I was driving home from work. A little sports car with little sports car tires came zipping down the avenue, but I was in a heavier and much slower vehicle, unable to zig when he zagged. After a boom, crash, zing, my car—with its brand new set of winter tires—was a crumpled, mangled mess.

The air bags erupted and a cloud of dust surrounded me. The horn started bleating at an ear-splitting level. Firemen from across the street were at my side before their truck arrived because we had crashed almost directly in front of the fire station. Within moments, I was eased out of the car and a very tall fireman was picking glass fragments from my hair while carefully looking at the gash on my scalp. In a surreal moment I realized that my life would never be the same.

At the time, my marriage was in big trouble and the car crash was just the beginning of a string of chaos. Not long afterward, I packed up my two teenagers, moved out of our home and filed for divorce. In May, my father was diagnosed with bladder cancer, and in June, my mother found a lump in her breast. As my divorce was being finalized, my parents were both in the midst of chemotherapy and radiation. My grandfather was being assessed for placement in long-term care, and I was doing everything I could to help. Meanwhile, I continued work on graduate studies and held a full-time job. It was a hard time, but I figured I would cope and get through it. I had to tough it out and suck it up. Then my doctor booked me for two surgeries six weeks apart.

In between those surgeries, a dear friend called me. "Come on over," she said. "I have a film I want you to see and a brand new bottle of wine."

We watched the film, and I thought it interesting, sure, but in no way could I do what those people had done. I did not have the power to bring on that level of profound change, I told my friend. There was too much negativity going on around me. Law of Attraction? Secrets? "Too much fuzz and not enough science," I said, and we talked on into the night in a way that only two friends can. With some tears and a box of tissues, she looked right at me and said, "I have faith in you. Look at the crap swirling around you right now. It's all you can focus on, right? Well, what can it hurt to try and focus on the things you want in a way that is like the one they talk about? Think about something as if you already have it; love as you wish to be loved; live in the way that you wish to live."

When I got home, I prayed for the first time in a long time—hard. It did make me feel a little better and over the next couple of days, I shifted those prayers from wishing and hoping to doing and living. I ordered two copies of the film and watched it again when it arrived. I shared the second copy with my friends and family to see what they thought about it and to get their opinions on human confidence, empowerment and their ability to create the lives they desire. Their reactions ranged from misgivings, as mine initially did, to overwhelming enthusiasm.

Soon afterward, my youngest daughter was contemplating college.

Her dad and I had always maintained that as long as the girls lived with either one of us, we'd pay for their tuition costs without having to worry about dormitory fees. The trouble was the university that offered what she actually needed was 3,000 miles away. Perhaps, I speculated, this was an opportunity for both of us. Nine months later, we headed off on our journey.

Now, I will agree that 3,000 miles is a long way to go for a "new start," and many changes do not require a move that significant. Change starts on the inside, in our hearts and in our minds. The catalyst is different for everyone and sometimes it takes a friend to help us realize we can really do things differently. My shift in philosophy and approach to life was as enormous as my physical move.

Since arriving here in our new home, I have met many kind, warm people and have made some great new friends. I am in touch with family and old friends from our former city and lots of them have been here to visit. I am so lucky that I have more work than I want. I am privileged to write, speak and offer support to people who are looking for direction on their own journeys. People have said to me, "Wow, that was pretty brave of you to make that break and move all that way." It felt easy in many ways though, because it was the right thing for me to do; it was a way for me to be where I wanted to be and to create the life I love. I have learned if you want something badly enough, you can amaze even yourself with the strength and wisdom that you have on the inside.

My favorite expression for years has been "carpe diem," which roughly translates from Latin to "seize the day." That's my motto, but it is important to note I do not mean it in just a simple way. I mean it like this: Seize the day and make the most of it; embrace what you have; create the life of your dreams and bring it alive. Don't wish you were living someone else's life. Truly live your life and, in return, you will be blessed.

Carpe diem.

Pam Robertson, Ph.D.

FROM SUICIDE TO SUSTAINABLE INNER HAPPINESS AND LOVE
Lora M. Bilger, Dipl. Päd

While writing this story, I'm riding a train from Germany to Florence, where a dear friend has recently passed from cancer. Tonight we will be gathering to share in a ceremony for him.

One week before my friend died he asked me to come see him. I canceled all my business appointments and made the long trip. When I arrived at the hospital, one of the first things he wanted me to do was to speak about my dying and after-death experiences. He must have known it was his turn very soon. Happily, I retold this story as I knew it would calm him and allow him to be at peace when facing his own death.

My death adventure was the last major one of a long series of unexpected and unusual experiences that had occurred for nearly 30 years.

As a young woman, I was miserable. Every part of my life was ruled by intellect and I was completely cut off from my feelings and emotions. Warmth and closeness made me feel terribly ashamed and I felt that life was a fight I could not win. At the age of 20, I tried to commit suicide.

As a 14-year-old girl, I threw away my deep childhood beliefs. At 16, I called myself an atheist and abandoned the church. At that time, my contact with people was tainted by control and mind domination. Inwardly, I felt lost and alone.

I loved intellectual discussions, philosophy and daydreaming, but on the practical side of life, I could hardly manage even the most urgent things. I was convinced that society and my parents had ruined my life and when I was criticized it devastated me.

To help myself and others, I decided to change my profession and train as a psychologist, social pedagogue, psychotherapist, coach and supervisor. Since then, I have had a series of spiritual experiences that have made me realize there is so much more than my brain. These experiences changed the attention and the direction of my life 180-degrees, making me look for a path that would work for me, uniting my own wishes with my Creator's. I'll only mention the most interesting ones here.

My inner shift began in 1984.

On a lovely, sunny afternoon, my first son was sleeping in his bed. While resting, I suddenly felt I was becoming smaller and smaller, being quickly pulled into infinite smallness, to a point where I disappeared completely. The force was so intense that there was no chance for control. Then the movement turned in the opposite direction. I was pulled from nothingness and expanded into infinite vastness at an ever increasing speed. I felt I was filling the whole universe, being filled myself, with this incredible force. This movement seemed to last forever. I was stunned with awe.

At this moment, I knew that eternity is to be found only in the Here & Now. I felt I was being called by a Great Life Force, as I had felt when I was a nine-year-old girl.

One week later, I found my true inner path. Or, did it find me?

During the birth of my third son in 1990, I witnessed another unusual experience. I felt a sudden swinging movement in a power and manner that reminded me of carnival rides in a swingboat. While swinging, I saw the brightest imaginable colors, accompanied by the most heavenly harmonies. I moved higher and higher until I reached the top and stayed there for what felt like eternity, looking into something white and indescribable. At that moment I realized this was what is called "nirvana." I could have stayed there forever, but my newborn son waited for me.

Here is the story I told my dear friend in Florence on his deathbed:

In 2006, while relaxing on my bed at noon, to my surprise I watched myself put my body in my own hands, laying it aside like one does with a toy one doesn't need anymore. I was wide awake outside and saw my body lying there.

Then I turned away and moved on, levitating more than walking. I knew I had died, yet it felt absolutely normal, factual, peaceful, interesting, light, free, bright and alert. I didn't experience any fear, worry, regret or any other emotion whatsoever. I consciously realized that I could still use all my functions as before, if not better. Light surrounded me and I knew intuitively where to go.

An inner voice made me understand why I was able to use all of my functions. In my regular spiritual practice, I had, bit by bit, let my soul come into all aspects of my being. Everything was in place.

As I walked, I heard desperate human voices calling loudly for help. While I knew it was not my job to help, I heard that voice again informing me that these souls could not move on because they had no orientation. During their lifetimes, they had missed the connection with their souls so they didn't develop what was needed on the "other side."

I had to come back, as my task here wasn't complete. This experience was meant to show me and you that death is nothing to fear, because it doesn't exist. Now I do not have to believe in it anymore—as I now know.

So, why am I telling you these intimate stories about my life? Since 1983, in my profession, combined spiritual growth and insights have led me to develop a unique approach that cultivates sustainable inner happiness, alert awareness, purpose, inner peace, love and freedom by learning how to distinguish between ego- and soul-motivation in our daily lives and how to help others move on to much deeper levels with joy. And this distinction is so important yet neglected by most of the Law of Attraction stuff. Without this, our souls cannot find their way into all of our functions and cannot find unity with God or Eternal Love. There is no other way to create these qualities. They cannot be bought.

I have dedicated my life to this work, supporting whoever wants to distinguish between their soul's life purpose from their ego's purpose and to learn how to focus on the soul's purpose, for meaningfulness in life.

Lora M. Bilger, Dipl. Päd

NOT BULLET-PROOF
John Assaraf

I have been blessed: At an early age I learned the value of my health. Plenty of people spend two or three decades believing they are "10-feet tall and bullet-proof," but at the age of 17, I was introduced to the reality in a major car accident.

For several months I had no choices concerning my physical condition. Then I started an intensive rehab program. Up until that point, my dream, like that of many other kids, was to play professional basketball. The dream still lingered when, at 21, I was diagnosed with ulcerative colitis. I was absorbing 25 pills a day, including cortisone enemas to help with the severe pain and discomfort of that disease.

It doesn't sound like the story of someone who is "blessed," does it? Yet, it is true, and the reason is simple. Long before it was too late and long before I could develop poor habits, I was shown beyond any doubt that God only gave me one body to hang around in. My job is to keep it in the best operating condition that I can. That includes both the physical and mental elements of the self.

I made that discovery when I was young enough to understand that my body is breakable. I decided that I would not be unable to enjoy the quality of my life due to my abuse of this miracle called a body. As I got older I also became aware of the spiritual side of my being. I learned how meditation and calmness allow me to be at peace.

So, today, my regimen includes a daily meditation to connect with the source that created me, along with a workout to keep this body in high gear. I play life to the fullest, and I want this vehicle to last as long as it can. My responsibility is to learn as much as I can about the latest and best practices to make this happen. Prioritizing my physical and mental well-being above work and social concerns allows me to take care of me first.

Is that selfish? I think not, for my belief is that everything we do is better if we do our best.

John Assaraf

WHAT IF MY LIFE IS PERFECT JUST THE WAY IT IS?
Monika Summerfield, M.A.

One morning, as I was driving to my yoga therapy empowerment group, a thought crossed my mind: What if my life is perfect just the way it is? I asked myself, "What is perfect? What if this life, the one I am living right now, is perfect?" Then more thoughts came: "My life is far from perfect. I work too much, my shoulders hurt, my neck is tense, our home is messy and we should make more money to be secure as a company. I'd like to have more time to myself."

I had these thoughts and knew they could be replaced. The human mind can come up with a million reasons why things aren't perfect. If we get "the deal," we feel stressed. If we don't get it, we feel we aren't moving forward in our career. If we agree to do something outside our comfort zone, we feel anxious or under pressure. If we deny ourselves the courage to try something new, we feel unfulfilled or depressed for the lack of excitement in our life.

So, back to my original thought: What if my life is perfect just the way it is? I let it sink in so I could experience its full meaning. If this were so, that would mean that everything now—everything I am experiencing—is in perfect order.

This made me think very differently about my life. Instead of feeling irritated or martyred, I felt grateful for the life I live. I trusted that my experiences had some meaning, even if that meaning was unpleasant or painful and deviated from my desires.

I decided to explore some of the challenges I felt right then. I wanted to see if I could find some truth in the thought that the shoulder pain I felt could be perfect—in the sense that it had a message for me. "Relax," it said. "Take care of yourself. Relax, you are safe. Breathe. Breathe some more. Breathe in your shoulder—breathe in love and breathe out pain. Continue breathing into the shoulder."

"Shoulder pain," I said to myself, "I can see the perfection in you. You have reminded me to slow down and take care of myself."

Then I moved to another thought: Worrying about finances for our counseling center. How could my worrying about this be perfect? This made me think of the learning, growth, responsibility and leadership this center and my position in it have provided. I noticed that things always work out somehow. Keeping the finances in mind might be helpful to our cause and, in that, is perfection!

I then thought about how I had learned to negotiate and compromise when people in my life were irritating me, so even this felt perfect in its own way.

The next thought I wanted to explore regarded the pressure and judgments I felt for myself. I said to myself, "Wake up, Monika. That is what you might have the most control over!"

I wondered, "Do I really?"

My mind said, "It's your thought that came through!" I then remembered our motto for personal growth at Diamond Center: "Coal can only convert to a diamond under pressure." So, any pressure I was feeling was converting me into more of a diamond and therefore, was perfect.

If my life was perfect just the way it was, then I should be happy, grateful, joyful and inspiring to others on an even deeper level. The lesson was to see and accept all those challenges as valuable knowledge for my own growth and healing, as well as the growth of others. I thought about it and it felt good. Even more so, it felt true. I felt gratitude and the deeper truth of it, so I decided to keep reminding myself of this thought. Suddenly, it was no longer about stress and negativity. I reminded myself to use the tools I teach my clients to use. The affirmations I teach in the empowerment classes help people identify with who they really are. So, I repeated to myself, "I am love. I am peace. I am freedom. I am power." Those values were already programmed into my body because I teach them regularly. So I was reminded and the wiser part of me remembered.

Dear reader, this is your invitation to uncover the meaning of your challenges, or what you might call your "problems." What would they lead you to do or change if they were part of a perfect plan? How would you think about your challenges if they were part of a divine plan? Could they be seen as supportive of your growth to become a diamond formed by the pressures of life?

What if the life you were leading taught you more depth and maturity, or more compassion for yourself and others? What if you could look at the hidden message in anything that makes your life feel less than perfect? You could be like the sculptor who chisels off all the sharp edges of the precious diamond that is your life and makes it smooth. After all, every thought is replaceable. Only your mind believes it and gets to decide how you see things.

I decided to continue thinking that life was perfect. I thought it every day and observed how I felt. My days got better the more I thought it and the more I believed it. Sometimes I would forget and get caught up in negative thoughts about my challenges, and then I would remind myself, "No, you are not a victim. How would you like to respond to this? You do have choices."

Another benefit I experienced was that not only did it change how I viewed the past and the present, but it also changed how I viewed the future. My choices automatically aligned with my desires.

With the intention of having a perfect life, I focus more on doing the things that make me happy, such as spending time with loved ones, meditating, enjoying nature, and inspiring and empowering others.

Yes, my life is perfect just the way it is!

Monika Summerfield, M.A.

SPIRITUAL EMPOWERMENT
Sant Rajinder Singh

When I was a young boy, more than anything I wanted to experience spiritual realms. Spiritual fulfillment has always been the core value in my family. My grandfather, Sant Kirpal Singh Ji Maharaj, was a Sant Mat Master, an enlightened being with an international following. I saw him meet continuously with seekers of truth from all walks of life, from the president of India to an unknown beggar. All persons were treated with respect and kindness by him.

Since Sant Mat's teaching profoundly influenced my world view, I found it natural that I had a hunger to travel into the actual spiritual regions as taught in this tradition. I wanted to know if my existence would continue after I took my last breath. I needed to prove to myself the existence of my soul and a higher power. I wanted to go beyond other people's accounts of the realms beyond this world, no matter how much I revered the source of that information.

I was familiar with the general array of reasons for meditating. Some, for example, want to relax their bodies and minds. Meditation was also gaining popularity for relieving stress; doctors were recommending meditation to patients to prevent illness or speed healing; coaches and trainers were promoting meditation to improve concentration and performance. This was good, but not good enough for me. I wanted more. What was the point of relaxing my body, which would ultimately deteriorate anyway? What was the use of relaxing my mind, which resides in such a temporary abode? I wanted a guarantee that my soul somehow would continue beyond the allotted span of body. I didn't want to attach myself to something as fragile and unreliable as the human body and mind. I wanted the power and the bliss of the soul. I wanted it *in* my lifetime, not afterward.

In the Sant Mat tradition, there is a sacred technique which involves contacting the inner light and sound current flowing within each person. The Master opens the spiritual chakra, which is the gateway into higher states of consciousness. This involves sitting in a comfortable position, closing your eyes and focusing your attention at a point known as the "third" or "single eye," or ajna chakra, located between and behind the eyebrows. To keep the mind still, five spiritually-charged words are given to be repeated silently, which helps the attention withdraw from the awareness of the body and the outer world. Thus, the attention can be focused on the vistas of inner light and celestial music. I wanted to use this to travel beyond the constraining physical reality and, instead, jump into the fountain of spiritual bliss.

At the age of 16, I experienced a loving, inner light far greater than any of this world. I also heard celestial sounds far more melodious than any music I had ever heard before. I rose above body-consciousness to discover I had an existence beyond my physical body. I entered the timeless spiritual realms. This was the first of a lifetime of phenomenal and exciting inner experiences. There are no words in the physical language that can explain such bliss and intoxication. In the same way, to say Niagara Falls is a waterfall does not begin to describe the power of the falls. To say Mount Everest is a mountain does not begin to describe its majesty. To say the Pacific Ocean is a large body of water does not begin to describe its volume. To say the Milky Way is a galaxy does not begin to describe its size.

Deeply and profoundly influenced by my inner contact, I dedicated myself to it. I meditated at every possible moment. I found inner riches greater than any I could possibly accumulate on this earth.

In my life, nothing could compare to spending a month with my spiritual Master before I left for graduate school in the United States. My Master put me into meditation every day and gave me personal instructions. He would ask me about my meditation experiences of inner light and sound, and the spiritual regions I was visiting as I rose above physical body consciousness to enter the realms of wonder, beauty and light within. I described to him my meditative experiences of wondrous colors and celestial sounds that do not exist in this physical world, and of an inner love and bliss thousands of times greater than any imaginable. He answered my questions, refined my technique and helped me soar higher and higher. After all, beyond this physical realm are the astral, causal, supracausal and purely spiritual realms. Each had increasingly more ethereal light and music. Each filled me with more and more love and bliss until reaching the ultimate experience of union with the one, and bathing in infinite ecstasy and peace. I came in contact with a source of knowledge from which all other knowledge flows. A love far greater and more fulfilling than any earthly love embraced me with open arms. I found at my inner core a strength and power that overcame any fear. There was joy so intoxicating that I needed no intoxicants of the world.

The spiritual journey is a journey beyond all others. Historically, enlightened people have realized themselves at the level of the soul and have taught others to do the same. I have found I am a traveler on a road that has been trod by many footsteps before me. The tracks have all been laid out for humanity by the spiritual pioneers who traveled this road and have taught about its intricacies.

Life can be thwarted by anxiety, fear and hopelessness. However, there is a source of fearlessness which can help overcome inner turmoil. Soul is immortal; it has the power to heal and inspire toward unimaginable heights. It alone holds the true key to unity and peace. Its qualities include unlimited wisdom and unconditional love. It is infinitely patient, waiting for undivided attention. This secret was uncovered by me on the journey into the spiritual realms. I had to pay attention to my soul: I had to focus on its manifestation and allow myself to soar beyond physical consciousness. I had to spread the wings of my soul and fly into the arms of the creator. Through meditation on the inner light and sound, I freed it from its shackles and helped it emerge into its glory.

Sant Rajinder Singh

MASTERING FORGIVENESS
Joy Pitts

Forgiveness is a virtue I was taught very early in life. It seemed somewhat easy when I was small, yet, as the seventh child, I often forgave my victimizer and appeared to free them to repeat the behavior. Therefore, I concluded that forgiveness transformed me into a doormat. As I approached adulthood, the goal of forgiveness became increasingly difficult. Many times I felt the scum buckets didn't deserve to be forgiven. I also held onto the opinion that the words, "I forgive you," would give them the license to take advantage of me. So I refused to give them this power. Being victimized was not my cup of tea. The kind of forgiveness taught at church didn't work well for me.

When I reached middle age in the mid-'90s, I began to read and attend study groups for a book called *A Course in Miracles.* The best part about forgiving, I finally learned, is you don't have to forgive anybody to his face. I went to seminars, took classes, attended workshops and achieved further success, but even after a decade of study, there were still some things and some people I could not bring myself to forgive. I desperately wanted to be able to forgive completely since enlightenment, inner peace and empowerment were my goals. Holding a grudge is like taking poison and waiting for the other person to die. This is not something I wanted to do because it eventually results in regret. Furthermore, until it is mastered, we are given the opportunity to forgive over and over again.

In my quest for self-improvement, I also learned I needed to forgive my worst enemy—myself. This turned out to be an ongoing struggle. Just when I feel like I've forgiven everything, either something I've overlooked pops up or a new opportunity to screw up presents itself. When this happens, I often use a valuable tool called a worksheet to get through it. It is working very well, clearing out cluttered areas and allowing me to receive new things in my life. And guess what? It makes me feel clearer and lighter, and an invigorating new energy fills the newly created space. It feels like a new lease on life.

The key to all of this is to insert a space so "forgive" becomes "for give." To practice with this, have someone you trust stand in for the person you want to forgive. Then, look him in the eye and say this sentence stem, "Thank you (his name) for giving me _____," then finish the sentence, and say what you need to get off your chest. Notice I made two words out of "forgiving." The first time I did this was with my good friend, Deidre, as a stand in for Grace, the person I needed to forgive. I looked her straight in the eye and sincerely said, "Thank you, Grace, for giving me the opportunity to stand up for myself so people will not walk all over me again. You can walk *with* me, but I will not let you walk over me any more." Use this technique and you will feel burdens lift and peace fill the space where they previously resided.

I once traced the word, forgive, back to its Aramaic root, "shbag," meaning "to cancel." According to the universal Law of Attraction, cancel is the perfect thing to do mentally in that situation. If you cancel the unforgiving thoughts and focus on the things you want, you will attract what you want. We are way too tolerant of mind-wandering and negative thoughts. Discipline is required in order to monitor and change your thoughts. When you change your thoughts, you change your life. In *A Course in Miracles*, the phrase, "choose again," is often used. If a negative thought is on your mind, you are simply instructed to choose again so you have the opportunity to choose powerful, affirmative self-talk. Applying discipline is a lot of work at first, but soon it becomes easy to cancel unforgiving or negative thoughts. Just say, "Cancel. Cancel," then think about what you really do want. This is a call to clarity. You must get very clear in your mind.

I struggled to forgive before I learned these techniques, but now it is easy to "for give" and "cancel" anything I wish to let go of and no longer want to allow into my life.

When you "for give" yourself, everyone and everything, you give yourself freedom and open your life to peace, joy, harmony, fun, abundance and love. This is empowerment.

This empowerment has brought me to living the life of my fondest dreams. Far from the corn fields of Indiana where I was born and raised, I now reside in Hawaii, my favorite place on Earth. I am so happy and grateful I learned to focus my mind to empower my life that I wish to share this with the world. When we forgive, we are empowered, and when we are empowered, we get a glimpse of eternity. Just the tiniest glimpse of eternity beats any other experience here on Earth. It brings inner peace, faith, hope and joy into the heart and soul.

Joy Pitts

POWERFUL SECRETS, A LIFE-CHANGING JOURNEY OF DISCOVERY
Cecilia Nannini

Discover 10 Powerful Secrets and the wisdom to empower every area of your life, creating the life you love.

An Open Mind
My first experience with speaking to a clairvoyant blew me away. I didn't know if I believed in clairvoyance or not, but I was curious. As publisher and editor of a lifestyle magazine, I decided to do an issue on "Clairvoyance, Spirituality, Alternative Medicine." How convenient! I could disguise my curiosity and fascination as "research" and people would not look at me as if I were crazy. After all, I had studied science at the university level, and I had a business degree—both very serious fields of study.

One thing the visit to the clairvoyant did was shatter some lifelong concepts I'd held that determined how I viewed the world. Any doubts I may have had about clairvoyants being able to "see" the future were completely eliminated. She told me in great detail about the present, as well as things that were to happen to me three years in the future. I realized my view of the world and my idea of time had to be completely re-evaluated. How could anyone see things that did not yet exist?

At this point, one thing became clear to me: I needed to approach life with an open mind. There were things I needed to find out about life, the universe and myself.

My Life Hits Rock Bottom
Shortly after my visit with the clairvoyant, my life hit rock bottom. I

was in my late 30s and lived in a modest, but comfortable, home in a well-to-do suburb with my partner. I had started a magazine publishing business so I could work from home. My intention was to start a family. However, my partner, being four years younger than I, was not so keen on the idea. He didn't want the extra stress of supporting a child. I knew I would need to prove I could still earn an income and look after our child, because having my children looked after by someone else was not for me.

The solution was to own a business I could run from home, with flexible hours so I could care for the children at the same time. Sounds perfect, right? Wrong!

Within two years, not only did I not have a child, but I didn't have a partner, a house, a job or any assets. I had lost everything. I had invested all my net worth into the publication. My partner bought out my share of the value of our house so I could invest the money into the magazine. The tension and stress of the business were causing problems in my relationship, and after 12 years together, we separated. I had to move out.

Although I had broken even on the sixth issue of the magazine, there was nothing left of my working capital to keep the operation going. I felt like I was pushing a very heavy wheelbarrow up a very steep hill. I tried everything I could think of, but it just wasn't working. I should have been able to do this. Where did I go wrong? I had to admit I had failed.

My Dark Night of the Soul
It was the worst time of my life. I was exhausted and I felt a huge loss. I felt alone and very scared, still owing creditors about $25,000.

I woke up in the middle of the night feeling I was at the bottom of a deep, dark well. I was so far down I couldn't see any light above. I was crying and I couldn't see how to get out. I even briefly considered suicide as one of my options, but I simply couldn't cause that sort of grief to my parents. I felt hopeless. I surrendered. This was my "dark night of the soul."

That night, something happened. I woke up a different person and things started to fall into place. Opportunities started to present themselves. A friend told me about a great job that seemed tailored for me. After seizing that opportunity, I negotiated with the bank for a loan to pay off the creditors. Information I desired seemed to come just when I needed it. At that time, Oprah was doing the *Remembering Your Spirit* series and inviting great, inspiring guests on to her show. I followed leads by buying books and reading everything I could. I was fascinated, amazed and inspired. I took courses in meditation and I was waking up, little by little, to an awesome world.

I had started my journey of discovery.

The Journey of Discovery Begins
Along this journey I have discovered powerful secrets: the Law of Attraction and the power of "now." I learned to distinguish between my ego and my true self—the observer. I learned how to listen and trust my emotional guidance system. I learned to accept that everything is as it should be. I was amazed when I learned about my life's nine-year cycles and how to work with these to empower my life. I discovered how to ask the universe for what I needed and to be patient while I waited for it. I learned to recognize when the deliveries came in, and take the appropriate action in order to receive them. Most importantly, I learned to be grateful for everything that comes into my life.

I now know that whatever we experience in our lives, whether desirable or not, we are responsible for it. I realize each of us has the power, if not the know-how, to attract what we want to experience. This is *amazing* to me. Why are we not all living this way?

I decided my purpose in life was to help as many people as I could with this life-changing wisdom, so they, too, can live the life they love.

My Love, My Passion

I now spend my time doing what I am passionate about, passing on all the secrets and techniques that have helped me. Through tele-seminars, writing and newsletters, I share everything that has worked for me—what steps to take, why they work and why they sometimes don't. I teach people how to improve skills to make these steps work every time. Whatever area of your life you want to improve, whether it concerns finances, careers, relationships, weight, health or parenting, this wisdom and know-how can be applied. On my Web site I offer free resources on how to start turning your life around.

I now have the life I have always wanted. In a period of five short years, I went from having nothing to owning a lovely home in a great location. I work from a glass-front studio at the back of my house overlooking a leafy garden and a lily pond while my golden retriever lies under my desk.

I make a living doing what I love, and, yes, my life allows me the flexibility to stay at home and look after my wonderful daughter. For me, life doesn't get much better than this.
I am living the life I love, and if I can do it, you can, too!

Cecilia Nannini

FROM THERE TO HERE, IT'S THAT SIMPLE
Melinda Day-Harper

"Everything should be made as simple as possible, but no simpler."—Albert Einstein

As I sit here on my porch looking out over the beautiful Texas hill country, the power of simplicity strikes me. A CPA by profession, I've always tended toward order. I suppose in some way it enables me to feel in control of something. I've spent 20 years of my life struggling to prove that order exists.

I lost seven family members from 1984 to 1987, including the tragic accident that took the life of my sister's husband of three months, the unexpected death of my father-in-law, the brutal murder of my father, the subsequent murder trial and my grandfather's massive heart attack shortly thereafter among others. Within a six-week period in 1995, my dear grandmother, Nan, had a stroke and died, my mom had brain surgery to remove a large tumor, and my brother was accidentally electrocuted to death. Yikes! The few details of those years seem truly unbelievable when I see them in print.

In that 11-year period, there was no time to grieve. I had funerals to plan, eulogies to give, family to comfort, night school, a job, a daughter to raise…. In short, I created a very busy and complicated life so I could hide from my emotions. This was out of fear, of course. I wasn't sure what would happen if I opened that vault in my head where I hid my feelings, but I was sure it wouldn't be pretty.

Of course, in my mind, it was all God's fault. How could he have allowed this many tragedies to happen to me? Because it's always about me, right? The one emotion I did allow myself to feel was anger. I relived those events over and over in my head, day after day, and shut God out; but today, I am so very grateful for the blessings I've been given including my family, my animals, my company, my friends and my peace. I wake up every morning in awe of the life I've been given.

How did I get from there to here? A very dear old friend of mine once told me, "God is a gentleman. He won't push Himself on you, you have to invite Him in."

I had to open my heart again and learn to trust that a benevolent power greater than I was in control and could do a much better job than I of running my life. By giving up my perceived power, I became empowered.

Okay, so it wasn't as easy as it sounds. I had to crash first and be stripped away of the ego that kept me extremely successful in business, but in little else. So, in His all-knowing way, He allowed me to be unemployed for six months, the only time in my entire life I had not worked full-time. I have never been so miserable as I was during those six months. I didn't know what to do with myself and the door of my vault began to open. It was very scary. I couldn't allow that to happen, so I once again buried my emotions by numbing them with alcohol. I actually began to pray again during those six months. Of course, my prayers were only pleadings for my own selfish desires accompanied by an occasional cry of help thrown in.

The year 2000 brought with it a wonderful job as CFO of a group of companies owned by a friend of mine. It was an absolute godsend, though it wouldn't be until 2005 that I was finally forced to deal with the prior 20 years of grief. I thoroughly enjoyed my new company and did an admirable job those five years, but occasionally my old deadly emotions would seep through the vault door.

At the beginning of 2005, all the old memories, anger and business came rushing back as I prepared for the first parole hearing of my dad's murderer. I wrote family members for their letters to send to the parole board and sent my own as well. I spoke with various people in the penal system to do what I could to ensure he wouldn't be paroled after serving only 20 years of a life sentence. This proved to be too much for me, but it was only after the board denied parole that I collapsed. I was finished. The alcohol no longer numbed my feelings and I no longer cared if I woke up in the morning. In fact, when I did wake up, I was frequently disappointed.

Again, God encouraged my dear friend to help me. He gave me time off to deal with my issues, the first one being my alcohol consumption in the evenings which impaired my performance during the day. I spent a month "clearing my head" in a rehab center. I had no choice but to learn to deal with my grief, my anger and my separation from God. There was nothing obscuring the direct line between Him and me anymore. It saved my life.

Putting my life back together was a one step at-a-time process, learning to trust God and keeping life simple enough to remember from where my "power" comes. During the first seven months of my sobriety, I had to move my mom to San Antonio as her health deteriorated. She died a month later in hospice care. Two weeks after her funeral, my sister made a serious attempt at suicide by overdose and was in a coma for two days. She would repeat this attempt a few months later, which left her in a four-day coma and with permanent disabilities when she awoke. However, I remained at peace this time. It was simple, really. At the first awareness of consciousness in the early mornings, I sent into the universe my gratitude for another day, for the life I've been gifted. That simple act started my day with my "God connection." When negative feelings crept in during the day, I paused, took a deep breath and offered up more "gratitude." The last thing I did before falling asleep was to again send my "gratefuls" to God. You know, it's really hard to be grumpy when you're grateful! Truly, it was that simple.

Today I am blessed to be the CEO of T-Zone Consulting, Inc., which I founded in 2006 to help others break boundaries and to be inspired to live their passions and purpose. I spend each day, no matter how busy it may be, in gratitude for all the blessings I've been gifted in this life. I know that today I'm being the woman God meant me to be.

Now *that* is empowerment.

Melinda Day-Harper

DEFYING GRAVITY
Ray Van Praag

You can succeed at business and life by turning your game upside down. There is little question that these successes can be brutal endeavors and finding the rung that will take you up the corporate ladder is often fraught with self-doubt and a maddening pursuit for fulfillment. So, how do you maintain equilibrium as you balance so precariously on each step in your climb to the top? Although there are no definite answers to this question some truths do exist. Once accepted and utilized, they can help you turn your life and your business game "upside down." Please consider the following truths that will enhance your life at home and in your career:

1. You win some and you lose some.
This is a basic idea that applies unconditionally to any game in life. Awareness and acceptance can help quench the fire of loss and will help re-engage your forward movement.

2. Logic and analysis are the enemies of natural awareness.
It is only when the mind quiets, the water calms and the clouds part that you can clearly see the best solutions.

3. Win more by doing what it takes to help the others succeed.
Win-win solutions are yours to create. Helping the other guy begets agreement and agreement begets cooperation. Cooperation begets teamwork and teamwork compounds the best solutions. This brings about positive growth. Positive growth defies gravity.

4. There is no substantive difference between work and recreation.
In all of his brilliance, James A. Michener once said, "The master of

the art of living makes little distinction between his work and his play, his labor and his leisure.... He hardly knows which is which. He simply pursues his vision of excellence."

What is your vision of excellence at work and at play? Since the master of life sees no real difference between the two, it's only a matter of making a simple switch. Treat your work as recreation and treat your leisure as work. That should help carve a few thousand feet off the size of your mountain, and it will make a refreshing difference in your climb, turning business and life into much more enjoyable enterprises.

5. Right now, in this moment, all is good; all is safe; there is no danger.
Nearly 100 percent of our negative notions, worries and fears are not based upon reality. They are directly connected to thoughts and experiences based upon our past or our imagined futures. In this moment, we have everything we need to enjoy our here and now. Any fears based on fact and survival will be handled without our help. We will act autonomically (and in the best possible ways) through our body's "fight or flight" mechanisms that have helped protect mankind from "real" danger for hundreds of thousands of years. Knowing you are fully protected, please feel free to remind yourself of the importance of being here, now and of maintaining presence of mind. Both can be acquired and re-acquired simply through practice and reminders.

Will the above "truths" really work to help you turn your own game upside down? Here is a guide to understanding that simplicity and reality work beautifully together. You can have a more glorious life simply by increasing your awareness of and going with the truth.

FALSE:
1. Winning is everything.
2. Logic and analysis make a winning combination.
3. For you to win, others must lose.
4. Work is not fun. By definition, it's a chore and that's why they call it "work."
5. Our knowledge of the past is our best gauge for determining our present and future.

TRUE:
1. We will always win some and lose some, regardless of how we play the game.
2. Allowing our own natural awareness to reveal itself is the winning gambit in life and in business.
3. When it comes to success and growth, the win-win scenario is the only gravity-defying solution.
4. There is no substantive difference between work and recreation.
5. The past is dead, the future is imagined. The present moment is our best, only and most powerful time.

I sincerely hope you take these statements to heart. I wish you a long, healthy, happy, fulfilling and loving life.

Ray Van Praag

PIECING TOGETHER THE JIGSAW PUZZLE
Michelle Tweedie

Snuggled in bed, dreaming in the early hours of the morning, I feel something is wrong. Am I dreaming, or is it real? No, it's not a dream. I wake up around 4 a.m., and reality hits. My head feels like a rock, and I feel an almighty thumping. I hold my head, thinking it is going to explode. Dizzy and sick, it is a real task to get out of bed to take medication. Tears run from my eyes as I feel frustrated and desperate.

Why is this happening?

Where do these migraines come from?

Why do I get them?

How do I get rid of them?

I feel so alone lying there. The pain takes over my entire being, and I am lost—lost for what to do.

From the age of 13 until 40, I lived with migraines and headaches. In my 20s, I had a headache, a migraine, a thick, buzzing head or an off-balance feeling for 25 days a month.

Most of my days were spent pretending that everything was fine, while quietly, I was taking several drugs to mask my pain. I was literally taking packets and packets of drugs per month. When my body got used to one drug, I would switch to another. My energy level was low and I constantly felt tired. I didn't want to appear weak, so most of the time, I did my best to cover up my headaches—but I couldn't cover the migraines because I would have to crawl off to bed, often for days at a time.

I married in my early 20s and had two beautiful children, Emma and Jonathan, but the marriage broke up when our children were toddlers. I did my best to be a great mother to my children, but some days I would awake with what I called a "doozie of a migraine." How could I cope when my children were bouncing and full of energy, starting the day with, "Mummy, Mummy get up!"? All I wanted to do was curl up in a ball and do anything to get rid of the pain. Some days were spent lying on the couch while my children were running freely.

Outside, I could see the beauty of the day; the shining sun, blue sky and warmth beckoned to me. If only I could get rid of that headache so I could enjoy the day. I felt like my freedom had been taken from me.

I felt this way on and off for 26 years.

For most of those years, I was shouting, "Please, please help me!" and hoping that someone would give me an answer.

Seeing doctors and natural therapists and taking different drugs and remedies cost me thousands and thousands of dollars. I kept asking the doctors, "Why is it that I go to bed feeling okay, and then I awake at 4 a.m. with a migraine?" No one could answer my question. No one!

Each time I visited a doctor or natural therapist, I always went with hope of acquiring a pill or remedy I could take to make it end. Back then, hope was all I had.

Although I held on to hope and it brought me out of my despair and frustration, it was not enough to find healing. I realized I had to put the power back into my own hands.

I had to take control of my life. This is when my life started to change.

I spent six years researching, reading books and listening to CDs, DVDs and lots of natural healers. It was like piecing together a large jigsaw puzzle.

First and foremost, I learned to look at myself as a whole. I was looking for only one cause for my migraines and headaches, but I soon found out this was wrong. Many factors need to be addressed when dealing with disease.

I first focused on the physical problem and, over time, I began to learn that life is more than physical:
    Mind—thought patterns, emotional health, focus
    Body—diet, stress, fitness, breathing techniques
    Spirit—Believing in yourself with faith and energy. Understand how these all come into play with overall wellness and happiness.

After hearing about mind-set in many different seminars, I thought I understood it, but then I realized awareness of our mindset and how it works is an ongoing process. This is what life is about. It is about continual learning.

When you change your mindset, your life will start to change!

Life became a challenge of noticing my language pattern as I became aware of how I thought and spoke. It was a real eye-opener and still is. Understanding centers more around what we are feeling than what we are thinking.

Noting diet and exercise are good, I also want to mention how hard my life was when living with the migraines and headaches and shouting "no" at them. While engrossed in pain, I failed to open myself up to the reality of being and feeling well. This was my wake-up call, changing how I viewed my life!

My days are different now because I have a wonderful, loving partner who has supported me so much over the last 10 years. I now wake up feeling excited and eagerly jump out of bed to begin the day. I have 10 times more energy than before, and yes, I have my life back!

My 12-year-old son recently said to me, "Mum, most of my friend's mums look so old, and you used to look old, but now you look young." This brought tears to my eyes. It was a reminder of how I used to be, and of my overwhelming feeling of thankfulness for not giving up. This turned the hope I had carried for years into belief and awakened me to the beauty of "living life." Life is meant to be fun.

I have a purpose now, and best of all, I have a passion. Always in my heart, I have loved helping others. My purpose is to take my journey of living with migraines and headaches, along with the knowledge I have gained, to teach others that they, too, can be well because well-being is our natural state.

My self-discovery and journey from hopelessness and despair, to feeling fantastic and happy, came with many insights. Most of all, I was pulling on my inner strength and courage, not giving up, and believing in the power of healing. I truly let go and accepted that "all is well."

Michelle Tweedie

TRUE WELLNESS
Sharynne Gambrell-Frazer

The turning point in my life happened in July of 2005 when my 77-year-old mother was admitted to the hospital. Mom was in her fourth year of dementia, but it was not life-threatening.

More than 40 years of prescription blood pressure medication had caused polycystic kidney disease. Unfortunately, there is no cure for this. The only sign or symptom is sudden death, and within one month of her admission, she died. The prescription drugs had ravaged her kidneys. The autopsy pictures showed that her kidneys looked like Swiss cheese, the holes in them allowing toxins to dump directly into her bloodstream and poison her.

I was with Mom, Dad and Binky, our cat, as I watched Mom slip away from us day by day. The only consolation was that we fulfilled her wish and took her home to be with her family.

Mom passed away within 36 hours of arriving home. I could see my life duplicating hers because I, too, had the medical issues regarding weight, high blood pressure and hand-crippling arthritis. To be brutally honest, it scared me to death.

My dad is currently 84 and in good health except for diabetes. He has strong fortitude. We added more living food to his diet and completely weaned him off sugar. He uses Agave Nectar as his sweetener now and I watch like a hawk.

With more than 30 years of experience in the medical profession—including the operating room—I have developed a passion for the human body. I have learned much about nutrition. It plays a major role in the quality of our lives, and no matter how badly we abuse our body, it has the ability to repair itself. Sometimes the repair comes in the form of a cure—other times, in the form of relief.

If you are currently taking prescription drugs, please read this biography carefully. There is help for you, but you must be willing to take responsibility. There is a whole new world waiting to be discovered by you. Try working with a holistic or a naturopath to control your cravings and help you detoxify from refined foods, meat, dairy and fish. As you detoxify, you will notice a dramatic shift in your taste buds. The foods you used to love to eat will not taste as good as before.

My journey into raw food is an evolution that my body has taken on its own. I have willingly followed—and now truly experience— health, energy and a vibrancy I haven't known since I was in my 20s. Listen to your body because it will tell you whether it wants to eat or not. I have learned to "eat to live" and not to "live to eat." Always remember that portion control is critical to any permanent lifestyle change. With living food, you don't starve yourself. You will eat delicious and decadent recipes—some so simple they can be prepared in 10 minutes or less.

Take control of your life. Come join us and experience true wellness.

Sharynne Gambrell-Frazer

WAKING UP THE PASSIONATE LEADER
Tom Brady

Empowerment is probably the most overused term and under-utilized concept in business. Why? Because an organization cannot empower people; individuals must empower themselves. This is exactly what I try to do for myself and those I love—family, friends and executive coaching clients. I try to get them to empower themselves and inspire others by their examples. My formula for this empowerment is: G + L + F = Joy. I call it waking up the passionate leader.

The finishing touches to this formula came to me in a series of my own wake up moments during a period in early 2007. At that time, my wife and I became empty-nesters, celebrated 20 years of marriage, enjoyed a successful business with more than 10 years as executive coaches and I survived my anxieties over my 60th birthday. I began by focusing my passions on making this my next best decade.

Not surprisingly and almost on cue, the shift began in April 2007 as I was preparing an annual presentation to a professional group with which I am involved. I love presenting every year because they are kindred spirits and always challenge me to go deeper into what I'm trying to teach. I had been playing around with a speech titled "The 'G' Word, the 'L' Word and the 'F' Word in Business and Leadership."

As I was editing my presentation the week prior, I revisited my personal mission statement. I felt at that time that a "Wake Up" moment was going to happen, but I couldn't find the words. As I was focusing on the G, L and F words, it hit me. The "L" word (love) was also about self-love, not just serving others lovingly. I modified my personal mission to read: "Igniting inspiration by enthusiastically coaching people around the world to discover the simple truth that loving ourselves leads to manifesting our passions and fulfilling our need for purpose."

However, the formula wasn't yet complete. All I had were G, L and F words. Upon signing in at the conference, I received a goodie bag, which included one of my favorite thought provokers, an Angel® Card. I love these cards because they can be used to set the tone for the day, week or the year. My Angel Card was "Joy." Without hesitation, the G, L and F words became the formula G + L + F = Joy. Joy, according to my "angels" at InnerLinks, means "approaching life with a buoyant attitude, light heart and unencumbered mind. Let joy lift your spirit and fill each moment." I even made joy my number one personal value!

By putting these words into my approach to coaching, it opens the door for me to inspire executives who are starving for a deeper sense of their own empowerment. One of my clients stated that his wake up moment in our coaching was the day I told him it was okay to use the word love in his leadership style. He knew at that very moment he was talking to someone with similar beliefs about people. From that day forward, he trusted me to take him on this journey.

That story illustrates how we continue to become more fully empowered. I'm not going to elaborate on growing up in a dysfunctional, alcoholic family; flunking out of college; doing and selling drugs; drinking; working myself out of my first marriage and eventually becoming sober in 1985. There were many people trying to get my attention during that time, but if you aren't paying attention, it's hard to hear the universe shouting, "Wake up!"

I started my big wake up with the help of Earl Nightingale and the co-authors he introduced me to while driving. He became my "audio dad." I remember him saying, "Five years from now, you will be the person you become from the books you read, the people you meet and what you think about." Earl's guests became my audio "big brothers" like Denis Waitley, Wayne Dyer and Ken Blanchard, whom I have had the good fortune to meet and thank. In 1989, I cried when a new voice on the cassette informed me of Earl's death.

Once I was paying attention to my many teachers, I was able to hear a song that now forms the basis of my unique coaching system for focus and clarity in our business and personal lives. To wake up, you need to ask the question, "What do I really, really, really, really want?" Then you can start singing, "Row, row, row your boat, gently down the stream." You know how it goes.

Having clarity and focus is what the "*XLR8 YOU!* Leadership Excellence" process is all about. If it can work on my hard head, then there is hope for others, too!

I call it "In Search for Adventure," which details:

What do You Really…
What are your top five passions?

Really…
Write them down and tell someone, anyone and everyone!

Really…
What actions will you take along the way that lead you to your passions?

Really Want?
How do they connect to your personal mission? Do you have one? Is it written down?

Now it's time to sing again. Ready?

Row, row, row your boat…
Acting on those passions with a coach—thus *"XLR8ing"* (say it three times fast!).

Gently down the stream…
Building on your strengths and unique abilities, getting in the flow.

Merrily, merrily, merrily, merrily…
Walk the talk of your personal values, a true source of happiness.

Life is but a dream!
Back to your personal mission—what are you dreaming about? Don't think small!

It all boils down to the formula. The God who is manifested in you, *no matter how you pronounce the "Ah" in your God*, allows you to "wake up." The more you are clear and focused with your God, the more you love yourself and will constantly be "Waking Up Living the Life You Love," in service to those who love what you do. That's when life is fun and it all adds up to pure Joy! Thus, G + L + F = Joy, the formula for passionate leadership.

The formula has led me to a deeper appreciation and love for my imperfect self—that guy who wasn't good enough until he discovered this formula for himself. By using and sharing it, I have grown tremendously as a coach, making a living and a life by living my purpose. I am grateful to those people kind enough to tell me that I have been part of their waking up to the passionate leader.

Now, that brings me joy!

Tom Brady

MAKE A DIFFERENCE, LIVE YOUR DREAM
Danielle Pampling

In today's hectic society, it's easy to get so caught up in your own trials and triumphs that you forget why you do what you do and what is really important to you. I realized not so long ago that it wasn't just me who was determined to find a better future for myself and my family; it's the dream of every human. Whatever you're looking for, you desire it for a reason.

Sometimes we want comfort and security, at other times we desire fun and happiness, but the fact of the matter remains: We all have dreams, even if we never speak them aloud.

For me the desire has been to make a difference in the lives of others—a big difference—and I wanted to touch the entire world, not just people I knew directly. I am committed to providing an environment and a life in which my children will see that anything is possible and they can have anything they want if only they have the knowledge, belief and heart to obtain it.

When I saw the passion in my children's innocent eyes and their excitement for each moment, I saw something in myself that had been suppressed. I was reunited with my own dreams and I began to remember what makes me happy. I felt at peace. My dreams had been inside of me all along, lying dormant. So I questioned the "me" I had known for so long and began to look for the "real" me underneath the stories, limitations and preconceived notions of society.

I began to ask myself: Who am I? What is my purpose? What is stopping me? Can I actually have everything I want? How does an uneducated, divorced, formerly-bankrupt mother of three finally have things go her way? After all of my life's ups and downs, how do I wipe the slate clean, create a new future, lead by example, express myself and fulfill my aspirations? The answer was simple: Just do it!

Here are some of the lessons I've learned along my journey:

Forgiveness

Let go of judgments, standards and that "right-or-wrong" frame of mind that keeps you stuck in a world of blame and justification. When you hold on to harsh feelings toward another, you only hurt yourself. You are drinking the poison you meant for someone else. Much of the time the other person doesn't even know or care what you think anyway.

Forgiveness is not only meant for others, you also need to forgive yourself. Do not be critical or beat yourself up over things you cannot change. It will separate you from others and from knowing yourself. When you learn to forgive, you will let go, give up attachments and accept things just as they are. You will have the freedom to just be, and you can give the special gift of freedom to others!

Appreciation and Gratitude

As I stripped away the chains of my past limitations, I began to see the beauty around me. Instead of focusing on where I wasn't, I began to appreciate where I was, then more of what I wanted began to appear.

Acknowledge and appreciate the skills you have, focus on your strengths and master your unique talents. Do not look for what you think may be wrong or dwell on what should have been. Be thankful for the wonderful life you have been given and cherish each moment as if it were your last. When you give praise for all that is good, you will attract wonderful things to your life. Go beyond a mere existence of struggle to a fulfilling life experience in which you realize that what once seemed impossible is possible now!

Do What You Want To Do
Only do what you want to do. I spent years trying to please others, trying to make sure everyone around me was happy. I thought that was what others wanted from me, but all I seemed to get out of this was stress and anxiety. When you do what makes you happy, you will feel healthy and happy. I notice when I stand up for what I want, everything works. I become inspired and excited and people around me are happy. You, too, can live a fulfilled and abundant life. You do this by following your heart's desire and standing firm in it. Do not be worried about what others think of you. Whether you realize it or not, you will be greatly admired for following your dreams and will inspire others along the way. Lead by example and live the life you love.

I have found in my experience when I live my life by these guidelines I am peaceful and happy. I am now discovering who I am. I say "discovering" because I know I have more to learn. Each day, as I am faced with new challenges, I see them differently than I did before. I see opportunities to learn and grow.

I love where I am in life and I am excited about what is to come. I have the power within myself to create the life I truly love. I have an international business that is rapidly expanding, and three amazing children who are also committed to making a lasting difference to the world. When I gave the love to myself that I was craving and began to see myself as a perfect human being, I was blessed with an extraordinary man to partner with in life. I am lifted higher than I had ever imagined I could go.

As I open my heart and mind, I realize I have always had everything I was searching for. All I had to do was open my eyes. My message to you is this: Believe in yourself, cherish the divine being you are, and know that anything is possible. Give unconditional love to yourself and to others, and you might be surprised with what you get in return.

Danielle Pampling

GETTING UN-STUCK
Kate Hyland Mercer

As humans, we tend to get in our own way. We struggle, get exhausted and give up. *I don't know what to do with my boss; I can't hit my sales number; I'm drowning in debt.* These are all phrases spoken by those who need to be empowered. Falling into chaos and feeling stuck is similar to falling into quicksand. Quicksand is an extremely saturated mixture of sand and water that can no longer support weight. Traction is not possible; balance is beyond reach; those who step in may never step out.

Although quicksand seems to suck its victims down and hold them there, it is neither a living creature nor a bottomless pit. In fact, quicksand is rarely deeper than a few feet and can occur almost anywhere if the right conditions exist. Quicksand is not the all-powerful force of nature it appears to be on the big screen. However, it is an excellent metaphor for a life in need of empowerment.

In the movies, we watch our heroes sink into pits of quicksand. Just before going under, they reach out and grab a tree branch or a rope from a friend to pull themselves out. When we fall into uncertainty, often our rope—the structure we need to help us out of our rut—is just beyond our reach. It seems that the more we try and the harder we commit, the more the goal evades us and the right choices become less apparent. As with quicksand, the more you struggle, the faster you sink. Fear and doubt creep in. They cripple you, preventing you from pursuing your goal no matter how badly you want it. During these times, we need to reach for a structure to help pull us out of the trap.

In his book, *Personal and Executive Coaching*, Dr. Jeffrey E. Auerbach discusses a structure I use on a daily basis to help myself, my family and my clients get out of the "quicksand" in their lives. It's called the G.O.O.D. Model and it is used to identify the desired goal, the obstacles that are preventing them from achieving the goal, and what options they have at their disposal. Once we see that we have choices, we can do something. We can then get back on track and take small steps forward on the path of hope and purpose. We feel more inspired, and that inspiration gives us what we need to create new behaviors using the G.O.O.D. Model—Goal, Obstacles, Options, Do-actions.

Take my friend Martha, for example. She was absolutely stuck, drowning in a pit of unbelievable responsibility. Over the previous year, she and her husband had taken their small business and launched it into a multi-million dollar venture. She was happy—she thought—but clients, vendors, employees and accountants were becoming overwhelming. She wanted to create a successful business, but now she felt trapped, as if it were out of control. She was afraid someone would discover she wasn't doing as well as she should be. She was falling behind in her bookkeeping. Even though it appeared as though she were "living the American dream," she was actually drowning in quicksand. The more work she did and the harder she ran, the further she fell behind. She was unhappy, and it was affecting many areas of her life. She needed a rope to pull herself out of the quicksand.

When I first introduced Martha to the G.O.O.D. Model, she laughed. While it might be a good idea for some, she said, she doubted that it could help with *her* problems. Although I understood, I asked her if she would humor me and give it a try. Desperate for a change, she decided she would walk through the process and she picked her biggest challenge: the backlogged accounting work.

Martha's goal was clear: she needed the books brought up-to-date immediately. She was nine months behind on recording the financial transactions of the company, and since she was the head instructor, she did not have time to sit in the office day after day to catch up on the required data entry task.

It was easy for Martha to identify the obstacles keeping her from achieving her goal. First of all, she had too many responsibilities on her plate. Secondly, because she was actually trained to do accounting, she felt she could not hire out the job. That would be a waste of money. The third obstacle was that she could never trust someone else with the financial details of her business. Finally, after some digging, we discovered that Martha didn't really want to do the accounting for the firm. She wanted to pursue her true passion, teaching the students.

The options that we uncovered for Martha as we moved through the G.O.O.D. Model included hiring out the job to someone (maybe even her CPA), getting one of the other employees to do it, delegating some of her responsibilities to make time in her day for the accounting work, or choosing to do nothing about the backlog. Once Martha was able to see that the problem had a definite set of options, she could stop worrying.

At first, Martha didn't like her options, but she began to see that she had choices and she felt hopeful. She could take responsibility and make a decision. She could see the small steps. If she chose one of the options and later realized that it wasn't working, she was free to change her choice. The structure of the G.O.O.D. Model was pulling her out of the quicksand and empowering her to do something positive toward her goal. Someone had thrown her a rope she could reach.

Martha's desired action was to trust the record keeping to her CPA. She was so inspired to move on her decision that she set the appointment for the CPA to come to the office and start working that very day. A huge load had been lifted from her shoulders. Recognizing that she had choices had empowered her; it inspired actions that allowed her to try a new behavior—delegating.

At times, we all need an outside influence to help us walk through the G.O.O.D. Model, but no one knows *you* better than yourself. Therefore no one can empower *you* better than yourself. Martha's story reminds us that when we have focus, purpose and choices, we are not victims of circumstance. No matter what life throws at us, we can slow it down and evaluate what we really have. Martha now disciplines herself to walk through the G.O.O.D. Model whenever she falls into a pit of chaos. She remembers that wrapping a structure around her goals allows her to get back on track and live the life she loves.

I challenge you to apply the G.O.O.D. Model to that sticky place in your life from which you want to escape. Grab the rope; Empower yourself today.

Kate Hyland Mercer

WAKE UP TO THE POWER OF LOVE
John W. Herbert

For you to understand my wake-up story, I have to tell you a little bit about what my life was like before.

I was born into this world with a strong dislike for religion; no one taught me this. In fact, my parents, though not fanatically religious, wanted me to go to the local Methodist church, but I was rebellious. I attended the church, but took my peashooter with me. During choir practice, I remember shooting peas at the choirmaster just to see how quickly he would become angry. It never took him very long.

By my early teens, I had come to thoroughly detest clergymen of any religion. Whenever I saw one, I thought, "Hypocrite."

When I was 19, I joined the British army, went to Hong Kong and, by the age 21, had married a beautiful Chinese girl. She was not only physically beautiful, but she also had a great personality. We had a wonderful 49 years together until she died in 2005.

In 1957, I was demobilized from the army and we returned to England. A couple of years later, several Jehovah's Witnesses called on us. As soon as they started to talk about the Bible I gave them a really hard time, but unlike the clergymen from my earlier years, my tirade did not faze them. They remained cool and loving. I realized they, too, had a similar attitude toward the clergy. I accepted a Bible study and became a Witness.

By the time I was 50, I had been in every position in the congregation and I had spoken in front of thousands of people. As an elder, I had been on several committees that disfellowshipped members of the congregation for sexual misconduct. It was this experience and other realizations that made me denounce religion. In 1984, I told the other elders I no longer wanted to be considered one of them, and I quit. I could no longer teach what I no longer believed.

After all those years of religion, I was no closer in my relationship with God. Despite knowing thousands of people, I had no real friends because I was an introvert. Even though I had a great job with Southern California Edison, I still came home at the end of the day with my jaws practically locked together. This pain in my jaw drove me to pursue my quest for truth without dogma. I bought a lot of self-help books and they helped somewhat. My request to God was, "I want to know the truth, the whole truth and nothing but the truth, so help me God. Please?"

That prayer was initially answered in 1987, but not with words. It came as an experience—a revelation of what life was really like and could be like for all of us if we chose to wake up and remember. It is impossible to fully describe. Some have said the experience is like a million orgasms going through the body simultaneously. That, however, does not really do it justice. All I can say about it is that it lasted for about half an hour and, while I was experiencing it, I was aware it was not just for me. I had done nothing that made me especially deserving of the experience. I was either in the right place at the right time, or more likely, my mental processes were such that they allowed the experience to happen. One beneficial result of this is I now have a totally different attitude toward priests, clergymen, monks and nuns. As an example of this, when Pope John died, I was able to watch the whole funeral service with total equanimity. When they kept referring to the Pope as the Holy Father, I would simply say to myself, "You are not my Holy Father, but you are my holy brother."

Since then, I have received a great deal of information, both directly from the source and from others pursuing a similar path. It is information that I desperately want to share with others. It is difficult to share unless one is already on the spiritual path to awakening, but my desire was to help others who had not yet started, or who were just beginning their search for the meaning of life. I wanted them to experience and come to the same realizations I had. My enthusiasm was so great that I think I initially put a lot of people off, so I came up with the bright idea of presenting it in the form of a science fiction story.

The first story I attempted to write was called *Return from Paradise*. I got about 400 pages written but didn't know how to bring it to a conclusion, so I scrapped it and forgot about writing a story for a while. My ego kept telling me, "You're no good. You will never write a book." However, I kept getting the feeling I should write. So I asked the Holy Spirit for permission to do so. As soon as I did that, the whole outline for the book came to my mind instantly. It was totally different from my previous attempt, and most importantly, I knew exactly how it would end. That book is called *The Perfect Choice* and is now available in stores. Many people who have read it have told me they thoroughly enjoyed it. It does not promote fear, but helps you to lose it.

John W. Herbert

GET BUSY LIVIN'… OR GET BUSY DYIN'
Suzi Broadwater

The monitor's glow cast a bluish pall over my distorted face, which was bloated from the greasy fast food and sweets I ate to sustain myself through the long days I spent at my computer. Feeling hungry again, I scanned my cluttered desktop for some sugary, comforting treat to quiet my nagging insides.

I blinked repeatedly, attempting to soothe my glazed and burning eyes. I raised my hands to stretch my cramping muscles. Instead, I was rebuked with sharp, biting pains piercing through my wrists. Unconsciously, I winced then continued tapping on the keyboard late into the night, as usual.

The pain grew to be too much, however, and I dropped my head into my cupped hands, tears leaking through my fingers. It didn't matter if I wept. No one would see my unhappiness or pain; they had all left hours before.

"I used to love my work," I sobbed aloud. "Why do I hate it now?" I flung open the desk drawer, rummaging for a pen. I began to furiously scribble down all the things I blamed for my misery.

As I went over the list that targeted outside factors as the cause of my problems, I saw what was happening. I was not in control of my situation. I was not in control of myself—eating, work schedule, exercise—nothing. Slowly, I began to realize what helplessness and hopelessness felt like.

I heard something I couldn't quite identify. It started low, like a whisper, and gradually and insistently grew louder and louder. The words

of Morgan Freeman from the movie, *Shawshank Redemption,* began
to echo in my head: "Get busy livin', or get busy dyin." I realized
that I had been blaming others instead of taking responsibility for
my own life.

With new eyes, I reviewed my list again, item by item. As I read each
one, a new surge of energy hit me and changed my life forever. I was
determined to change my thinking and my way of life. I recognized
that I was responsible for every aspect of my life. I had a choice
between blaming others and feeling hopeless, or choosing to take
control of my life. I resolved to make some new lists.

Each list started with the words, "How can I...." What happened
next was astounding! Like magic, my lists filled up with unimaginable answers. I immediately felt a rush of positive energy and began
thinking of ways to overcome the challenges I had identified.
Amazingly, the problems transformed into inspiring goals before my
very eyes!

I wrote and wrote and wrote. The more focused questions I asked
myself, the more answers I uncovered. My mind had created incredible possibilities. I felt a new sense of control over my life, and it felt
great! That night, I went home with a new feeling of hope.

The next day, I woke early enough to write down goals for my day. I
found sources of information and encouragement online that helped
me stay the course of action I had identified for myself. I bought
audio books on leadership, management and personal effectiveness. I
listened to the CDs every day on my hour-long commute to and
from work—even during my lunch breaks and while running
errands. The wisdom and inspiration drifted into my ears and pene-

trated my thoughts. I scheduled weekly self-development meetings for my team and shared my newfound skills so that they, too, could increase their personal effectiveness.

I now knew why I had been exhausted and weary. I discovered why I had been passed over for a promotion. I learned more ways to persuade and influence. I focused on solutions rather than problems and began to use facts to determine my next steps instead of using gut feelings or beliefs. I knew with certainty that I needed to continue feeding my mind for the rest of my days if I wanted to live a meaningful and rewarding life.

The more I learned, the hungrier I became for more information because the results were so wonderful! It all came back to the "granddaddy" Law of the Universe—cause and effect. I attended seminars, surrounding myself with groups of people who had positive and successful attitudes, and I modeled mine after them. Each time I followed the models, I experienced positive results. I'm not suggesting that I didn't make mistakes anymore—oh, no. I made even more mistakes than before. The difference was that I quickly learned the lessons from them, adjusted and moved on without taking them personally. Failures became the stepping stones on my pathway to success.

My life changed dramatically, seemingly overnight. One day, out of the blue, I was asked to manage a challenged area of the company because the leadership team now had confidence in my abilities. The most amazing result, believe it or not, was that the excruciating physical pains that had once nearly consumed me had all but disappeared! I had strength, determination and self-discipline within me now, and I stayed on track by eating healthy foods, exercising and taking supplements.

As I applied more successful methods and witnessed positive results, my passion grew exponentially, and I had to share this information with my co-workers, friends and family. Each time I explained what I had learned and saw it help someone else, I found my own desires reinforced and the resulting changes were so satisfying that I knew this is what I wanted to do for the rest of my life. I loved learning and helping others to learn.

I am now living the life I love, I am a Brian Tracy Focal Point Coach. For the rest of my days, I can use my mind and heart to help others experience the joy and success I now feel. In fact, my commitment to helping as many people as possible compelled me to write this story. I love sharing hope and inspiration with those who are facing challenges and obstacles or seeking purpose in their own lives.

The best part of my experience was learning to support my children with wisdom and encouragement. All three have sampled the passion, and now they thirst for the same success I have found. They are starting businesses of their own and pursuing dreams with zeal and knowledge. Many of my siblings and extended family have shifted their focus to their own visions and dreams as well.

A thought from my mentor, Brian Tracy, resonated deeply with me for many years. It has shaped my legacy. He said, "If you raise your children to feel that they can accomplish any goal or task they decide upon, you will have succeeded as a parent, and you will have given your children the greatest of all blessings." I want my children to have that blessing, above all else.

If asked for advice that would trigger similar changes for others, I would advocate taking responsibility for every aspect of your life.

Begin living. Wake up, and live the life you love!

Suzi Broadwater

LISTENING FOR GOD (FROM THE WAKE UP LIVE MOVIE)
Zachary Levi

My "Wake Up Moment" was when I realized how much God loved me and that there were things in my life that I wanted to do and things I felt like God had made me do. He wasn't keeping things from me because he was mad at me, he was keeping them from me because he knew that I wasn't ready for them. When I realized that, and when I realized that he wanted to bless me with those things, and I was getting my life together, then it all started falling into place. And so, my "Wake Up Moment" was knowing God's love.

So I would just tell young professionals of any kind to make sure you know why you want it. Is it because you really love the art of it, is it because you're really into the fame and the fortune? Know your motives as best you can, and know your passions as best as you can. If you are really passionate about it, you will go forward and succeed. You know, it's almost not even a choice.

So, it's not as if you're asking, "Should I be an actor?" It's "I have to be an actor, or a musician," or whatever the case may be.

But you also have to know that this may not be what you are ultimately supposed to do. Maybe it's just something you're supposed to pursue for a time that will bring you somewhere else. It should never be about who you are. It doesn't define you. You could go off to be the next Wolfgang Puck, but you never would have found that if you hadn't come to Hollywood and tried to be an actor. So always be open to wherever God is taking you.

Zachary Levi

WAKE UP CALL
Laura Jelenkovich

For a few seconds I could not hear or see anything except two giant icebergs floating on the surface of the Arctic Sea. Then the chilly air and loud clapping from the beach brought me back to reality. The word had spread quickly aboard the cruise ship that "the crazy Italian was going for an Arctic swim."

I was standing on a slippery rock, wearing a red, long-sleeved shirt over my swimsuit, a pair of gloves and yellow rubber boots. I was ready to dive! Nearly a hundred eyes were stuck on me, waiting for the moment of truth.

I felt like a rock star getting ready to perform an unforgettable show. "Okay, this is what's gonna happen," I said. "You have to count very loud from one to three and when you say three, I'll jump into the water." A big applause sounded and it seemed even polar bears somewhere were joining in.

Then I did it, very quickly and without thinking. It was so cold I felt like my entire body was cracking, but I had never felt so alive in all my life.

Later, while defrosting in the sauna, I thought, "Receiving a death wake up call is the worst awakening possible." You lift up the receiver in complete shock and there's only grief on the other end. You try to call the reception desk to tell them they have made a mistake, they called the wrong room number, but the receptionist always says, "I'm very sorry for your loss. No mistake." Panic sets in. With a trembling voice, you say, "What? What should I do now?" The distant voice answers, "Call the life desk for more help."

Five years ago, the call was about my mother and part of my life ended with hers. I called the life desk crying and asked, "What should I do now?" They just said, "Start living."

In the beginning, I thought it was the dumbest thing I had ever heard. I didn't know how to go on for even one more day, but I couldn't lie in bed forever, dropping my weight to nothing but bone. So I decided it was time to follow the advice of the life desk; I started living.

I bought books about mental training, spiritual growth and meditation. I found enough strength to earn my law degree only three months after my mother's death, even though I didn't remember how. The lesson I learned was not to waste a single moment of my life, it is too precious and fragile. That's why I decided to put my degree in a frame and follow my dream of being a photographer. My world almost exploded!

I started traveling around the world, seeing beautiful places and meeting special people. I touched nature and the hand of dying children in Africa; I heard waterfalls and cries of desperation.

I realized we're all connected: the rich and the poor, humans and animals, my small world and the Universe. I grew up. I became a woman—a happy woman. I made some exhibitions of my work and talked to more people than I could count. All of a sudden, I wanted more. I wanted the life of my dreams, and I remembered from the books I had read that the only way to get it was to think about it.

I have wanted to be a writer since middle school, but I believed I could only write short stories and that I wasn't good enough to write a full book—I was wrong. Thinking about a book led me to complete it in only a month. Each chapter flew into the next. They all came together, fitting perfectly like they were written by someone else.

Still, it wasn't enough. I considered more education, so I attended a marketing workshop in Miami where I met someone who changed my life—someone who taught me I could be rich. After that day, I studied to be a business consultant. People come to me for advice on good estates for sale, for short-term investments, for art purchases, for Web site construction and marketing counseling. Everything came so easily, I'm still not sure exactly how it happened.

The only thing I know is when somebody asks me for something, I'm sure I'll find what they are looking for. I think about it, visualize it and realize it. It works every time. Some time ago, I wanted to buy a painting of an author I had loved since I was a child, but I had no idea where to find one. So, I sent a message to the universe that sounded something like, "Okay, I want that painting. Now that you know it, find it for me. Thanks." I visualized it hanging on my wall while I spent time on my sofa just looking at it. After two months, a man knocked to my door asking for a Web site for his art gallery. Guess what? He had the painting I was looking for, and now it's mine! But he did even more for me: he started selling my Fotostorie™ and now I'm enjoying success as an artist as well. I do so many things, but I still have time for myself. I'm happy, what can I say?

When I received the death wake-up call, I never thought life could be so good again. But you know what, your life can be even better than mine, no matter who you are, what you do, or what has happened in your life. Don't wait for a painful wake-up call to live at your best. You can have the life you want now. Just remember, don't dream—think.

Laura Jelenkovich

IT'S ALWAYS LIFE
Dr. Ted Cole

Would you like to know the secret to life? Here it is: Learn. Grow. Love.

If that seems like more than one secret, then put them together. They work either way. If you want to live the life you love, then you have to start with the here and now.

Pretty simple, huh? The devil, of course, is in the details, and that's where life gets tricky. You need to know a few other things in order to be able to use that secret.

The first thing you need to know is that we are all damaged. All of us have emotional damage that forms the core of who we are, how we think and how we act. It provides the very framework of our personality.

Second, by its very nature, this damage remains mostly hidden from us. We are only able to see the fringes, like shadows out of the corner of your eye. You know that something isn't quite right, but you just can't put your finger on it.

This damage usually occurs very early in childhood, when our defenses are low and our trust is high. It's often done by those closest to us—our parents, siblings, grandparents—but don't blame them. They're in the same boat you are, just trying to cope with their own unseen damage and choices. It's not any easier for them, as anyone who becomes a parent finds out. We do the same thing to our own children and the circle continues until someone fixes it.

The third thing we need to know is we cannot repair the damage by ourselves. We require the help of others to fix things. Other people act as our mirrors, and we are theirs. How often are you able to clearly see the mistakes of others, yet can't seem to get a grip on your own? This is the case for all of us. So, we must look to our mirrors to see what reflects back to us. In order to benefit from the mirror of others, we have to accept that we have flaws and be willing to take an honest look at our reflection. On top of that, we have to determine if others are truly reflecting us, or might they have another agenda and are reflecting something at us that is really their own problem? Things get a lot tougher here, don't they? We have to take a long, hard, honest look at things to find the way.

Here is where the secret comes in. First, try to learn something. Don't view things as an attack upon you. Control the impulse to lash back. Break the cycle; ask questions, get feedback, think it over. Look inside yourself to see the truth. Find those people whom you trust to give you as honest a mirror as possible and do the same for them. They need it as much as you do, and everyone benefits.

Next, use what you've learned to grow. If the mirrors tell you that you are too critical, listen to what you are saying to others. Record yourself and listen to it with an open mind. Ask yourself tough questions: What does being critical accomplish for me? How does it affect others? Is there a better way? If so, start to incorporate other words and vocal tones into your speech. Turn your critical approach into a supportive approach. You probably have a lot to share with others, so make sure that it can be recognized and accepted. Help others learn to grow.

Finally, always have the feeling of love in your heart, and work from there. Love is truly the most potent of all emotions. I know it's not easy. We are human, not perfect beings. Love helps us accept the limitations of others and ourselves. After all, love includes the love of yourself. This is where you must begin. If you can't love and accept yourself with all of your flaws and weaknesses, you will never love your life.

Concentrate on the things you do well and that give you pleasure. Take stock of your abilities and interests. Be realistic. Ask others what they observe about you and what they think your strengths are. It's all a matter of perspective. Some of us have great abilities, and others only small talents. That's okay. I run a large medical practice, and I tell my employees that there are no unimportant jobs and there are no unimportant people. Each of us has a vital role to play, and everyone depends upon everyone else to do their part.

Look at your attitude. How do you view someone doing a lesser job than yours? Do you have jealousy or contempt for someone in a position of authority? What is your opinion of your own station in life? Where do these beliefs come from? This takes some tough honesty, but it's essential to answer these questions in order to find your way.

Now you can really look at living the life you love.

First: Are you living? Second: Are you loving life? If you answer yes to the first and no to the second, then there's a problem.

What is it that you don't love about your life? Go back to the secret: what are you learning in your life? We are where we are for a reason. We are here because of our choices and actions. Sometimes those choices don't turn out like we planned or hoped. This is an excellent time to learn.

The secret is to love ourselves and our lives *now*, rather than rage against the elements. This is where growth comes from. This is when true change will start to occur. We might wish it was different, we might wish we had made better choices, but here we are. Don't dwell on it; it locks us in place. Rather, accept your choices and the consequences. Recognize their purpose. Love yourself for what you have done and for where you are. Remember that the journey never ends and the destination is not final. Love your life wherever it might be.

It is fitting that as I write these words I am in the middle of great personal turmoil and change. I am facing challenges that will affect the next 10 years of my life and then some. Yes, I am using these same principles as guidelines for my own choices and actions. As you read these words, most of these issues will have been resolved, and I will be entering a new phase of my life and loving every minute of it. I wish the same for you!

Dr. Ted Cole

SALES: EMPOWERING YOURSELF AND OTHERS
Joy Porter

What I thought was a way to earn money has become a mission for me, a way of life and a way to connect and serve. Every day, every appointment can become a sacred space to empower and be empowered.

My early years and education were spent in the arts, film and TV production. It was fun and "prestigious," but didn't really pay the bills. I soon discovered my enthusiasm for ideas translated very well into selling products and services. Just as I had touted the latest art show or encouraged a film production, I could share a product with others and found they would buy it from me. Wow!

I went into sales strictly for the purpose of paying the bills. It was a temporary fix until something "better" came along. However, when my mom got sick, I became the breadwinner for both of us. I was in a position where I had to make more money, and fast. My mother and I were in survival mode and I needed to step up to a bigger game.

It was during this period of my mother's illness and urgent financial need that I experienced some intense awakenings.

I had made the commitment to her (and to myself) that I would find a way to help us get through. I realized that I could earn larger commissions if I went into direct sales. So, I chose a product and business in which I would visit people in their homes. I had previously sold over the phone or at trade shows, but going into someone's home is quite different. There is no phone between you, no

Internet and no distance. You are in the moment, at the moment. In the beginning, I was desperate for money. The bills were piling up and my mom was looking to me. Sometimes I didn't know how I was going to afford the gasoline to make it to an appointment. I was the one holding people up at the toll booth scrounging for change in the car. The pressure was intense and made for a difficult start.

I needed to make sales immediately and when I didn't, I became angry. At first, I was upset with the customer for not understanding that the product was perfect for them. Then I was angry at myself for not being the perfect salesperson and closing the deal. I was also angry that I couldn't provide for my mother the way I wanted to. In general, I became very critical of myself.

As I began to search for reasons why I wasn't succeeding, I first looked to what I thought was my poor performance. I studied the books of gurus and sales professionals to improve my presentation and to learn closing skills. I'm glad I learned most of those sales techniques, mostly to stop using them. They helped in some ways, but not enough.

Fear and desperation were clouding my life. I needed refuge from the stress, so I began to read and study spiritual matters, leading me to learn about forgiveness. Yes, forgiveness for those who didn't buy, but mostly forgiveness for myself and for my mother for getting sick. Slowly, I began to be kinder to myself.

As the cloud of resentment lifted, I began to really see the people sitting across from me during my appointments. I began to connect with them and listen to their concerns. I could relax and enjoy myself in that moment. That's when things began to change in all areas of my life.

I found that being in sales was not just about the money. It was a way to learn about myself—my weaknesses and my strengths. Selling was allowing me to earn an income, but I was also learning about people. More importantly, I was learning how to care.

When I stopped being driven by earning a commission, and instead began to focus on helping the person in front of me, everything turned around. I went into the appointments to help the client first. I would do the best that I could in presenting the material and would not beat myself up afterward. I would do the right thing for the client, even if that meant admitting that I did not have the right product for them.

It's been years since that experience and I've been continually learning and growing. Now I can say that I truly enjoy selling. It's not just a job or a way to make money. I'm not waiting for something better to come along. It is a way of life for me. I consider it a gift that I can connect with people and help them in some way.

I have found many times that a sacred space is created between me and the prospective clients. They share their hearts and their needs and I respect their trust by telling them the truth. I trust them to tell me how I can help. Then, I do my very best. The bond that is created allows us to empower each other.

Sales and selling is empowering for both parties when caring for another means sharing a solution or serving a need. It is empowering to provide a product to make life easier or help a business run smoother. I love helping people achieve their goals.

It's also empowering when the client understands I am coming from a place of service. This allows them to relax in order to understand the information that is being shared. With an open mind, a person can make better decisions.

For all of you who buy things from salespeople, and to all of you who sell, thank you. It's through selling and serving that I have seen many lives empowered and changed—all because one of us has "made a sale."

It has been a part of my spiritual awakening to understand that, day by day, I earn my living by caring for others. Selling connects me with people and allows me to find ways to serve and empower others to live their life to the fullest. This process has helped me grow personally and professionally.

Sales has empowered me and has become a type of spiritual practice.

Joy Porter

I WILL NOT LEAVE THE RING!
Rogeema Kenny

My story begins many years ago at what was to be my first of many major martial arts tournaments. It was the South African National Karate Championship. After taking the plunge and venturing into the world of competitive karate, I had proudly made the provincial team and was ready for my first national fight, but my inadequate preparation would soon put me at a great disadvantage.

During the first fight, I quickly realized I had not trained nearly as hard as I should have. I lacked the experience needed to fight at this level and I'd previously had no idea what to expect.

Out of nowhere, I was hit with a hard, uncontrolled punch to the face. It split my lip, made my nose bleed and severely hindered my sight. I wasn't even sure if I still had all my teeth.

I was totally overwhelmed and decided to discontinue the fight immediately, which would eliminate me from the entire division. What I hadn't realized was I had, in fact, won the fight since the only point that had been awarded was the penalty my opponent received for hitting me with an illegal shot. I had quit while I was ahead. How could I possibly do something so crazy? I left the ring in tears, but the physical pain I was feeling would pale in comparison to the feeling I had when I realized I had given up. How could I give up in the middle of a fight? That goes against every code in the martial creed!

The feeling of failure haunted me for weeks, until the day I decided I would make up for it the following year. Achieving this would require work, practice and an intense discipline far beyond what could be drilled into me by even the greatest of masters. This was something I had to find within myself.

I first had to make the provincial team again in order to qualify for the national tournament. I not only had to work on my fighting technique, speed and physical fitness, but also my mind, psyche and focus. I had to be mentally tough—tough enough to withstand absolutely anything that could possibly be thrown at me.

The next few months were a fascinating journey as I prepared myself for the challenge. I trained with the squad and if there was nobody to train with, I worked the punching bag or practiced in the mirrors. When training with a partner, I had to choose wisely, a partner who would not go easy on me because I was a girl. That would be the biggest disservice my partner could render me.

Finally, the big day came. I was about to face the challenge that had been an entire year in the making. *I had to step up and claim my victory!* All the sweat and hours I had put in seemed to have been worth it. I was on a roll—a winning streak. Then came the ultimate test.

I was again hit with a punch to the face. This time it sent me to the floor. It was an even harder hit than the previous year and I was down for the count, barely conscious of my surroundings. All I heard was the referee counting: *"1…2…3…."*

I then realized this was the moment that would determine my failure or success. Once he counted to 6, if I was still down, it would all be over. I would be disqualified. Even if I could not stand on my own two feet, I had to get up.

I stood up and nearly collapsed again, letting the medics do their thing. The problem came when they advised the referee that I was in no condition to continue the fight.

When the referee asked if I wished to continue or stop, I promptly informed him that I would continue. He strongly advised me to retire and explained the risks involved in continuing. None of that mattered to me. I refused to listen. I wasn't interested. I had come here on a mission, and nothing and no one would stop me from fulfilling it!

There was a fire blazing in my eyes that told the referee, without the shadow of a doubt, that he was wasting his time. Nothing would get in the way of my finishing that fight, no matter what the outcome was.

They allowed me to continue on one condition: one of the medics would be on standby at ringside to assist if anything went wrong. Thankfully, nothing did.

I lost the fight, but was not eliminated, and went on to win every single fight that followed through to the end of the division—a feat that earned me second place in the country.

It was the greatest feeling in the world—the feeling of true victory. Not victory over any external opponent, but victory over myself and the voice inside me that said, "*Stop! It's painful. It's not worth it. It's over. You're down!*"

It isn't over until you decide it is. You are never defeated until you give up. I did not allow anyone—including the referee and the medics—to tell me that I was not going to continue.

The victory over your own, self-inflicted limitations is the greatest of all. I know this because I've since won gold medals in bigger tournaments than the one I just described, yet the feeling couldn't compare. Winning is always an amazing, indescribable feeling, but the silver medal I earned in that fight stands above all the rest for me.

This is a lesson I've carried with me ever since that day, more than 11 years ago. It is a lesson I will never forget for as long as I live. It is the force that drives me to succeed in everything that's important to me. It is the force that drives me to do what it takes and to persevere when things look bleak. It is the reason for my success.

This lesson is what fuels my burning desire to help as many people as I possibly can to imagine possibilities beyond what they can see right now and to live a life beyond their wildest dreams—to prosper. Today I am immersed in a business that, by its very nature, allows me to do exactly that. I am eternally grateful I learned this great lesson in persistence and perseverance early in life.

Let your passion drive you to the greatness that is yours for the taking. Let nobody—not even yourself—ever stop you from achieving it!

Rogeema Kenny

WHERE DO YOU START?
Lee Beard

I had the most difficult time writing this reflection because of the conflict I feel when I hear the word, "empowered." I believe anyone can succeed at whatever he or she really wants to do. However, I have had people remind me that many factors can alter our paths to success.

I think of discipline and motivation as being internal, while empowerment seems to be an external influence. Yet, we are also empowered by the support of a team, a teacher, a mentor or a friend. We are empowered by the knowledge we get from reading or listening to informational material. Once we know how to do something, we are empowered to take wise action.

I know how excited I get when I figure something out or someone shows me how to do something. It removes the mystery and allows me to proceed. It doesn't have to be a huge revelation to be encouraging.

I really enjoy training and teaching. My wife says I am quite good at it and she would know better than anyone. I enjoy seeing someone make progress in his or her life, whether it is in a family relationship, a business or a career. That is the real joy I get from publishing authors in the *Wake Up...Live the Life You Love* book series and the *7 Secrets of Living the Life You Love* program, which was developed from working with some of the most successful people I've met along the way.

I have been collecting wisdom and insights in my journals for many years by writing what I feel God is telling me. It has been a great encouragement to my family and me. When I listen to God's guidance, the plans seem to be easy. However, when I get off track and stop listening, things never work out. God's path is empowering.

One example that comes to mind is when I got the desire many years ago to purchase a certain luxury car. The one I found was white with a red interior and it was sharp! I feel my ego got me into that car, which turned out to be an unwise purchase. A few years later, I wanted a sports car and the one I found was white with a red interior. I did not want to make the same mistake twice, so I dedicated the car to God and put a Jesus license plate on the front as a reminder. When I had something go wrong with the car, like a flat tire, I would just say, "God, you have a flat." It was empowering and liberating to put it in His hands.

Empowerment comes in many forms and at various times in our lives. I recently found a yellowed piece of paper on the bulletin board in my office closet that empowered my day and encouraged me when I read it. It read, "You are My child! Do you know what that means? It would be good to study what it means to be My child. All power is available through the Holy Spirit. All resources are available from 'Daddy.' All strength, all wisdom—everything you need is available through Me."

I encourage you to be empowered. Take your desires to heart, listen to the guidance of God and create your very best life by looking to the future for all of the possibilities He has for you.

Lee Beard

AUTHOR INDEX

Addams is a diabetic who believes that a Type II diabetic can have a major impact on the course of his diabetes. Addams has been a certified public accountant for the past 30 years. He graduated from the University of Washington in 1975 and from Wingate College in 1963. He enjoys traveling throughout Asia and would also like to travel to South America.

Address: 201A SW 153rd Street
Seattle, WA 98155
E-mail: garyaddams@webdiabetesclub.com

Akins is donating a portion of the proceeds from the sale of this book to Autism Speaks, Make a Wish Foundation, Special Olympics and the American Cancer Society. Geoff's gentle nature, humor and gift of rapport with children (and the young at heart) have delighted audiences worldwide. He presents his inspiring Bubble Wonders show over 300 times a year at fundraisers, schools, libraries, churches, synagogues, mosques, museums and other events all across the nation. Visit the Web site and see the Square Bubble!

Motivational Edu-tainer, Author and Speaker
Telephone: 847-668-2808
Web site: www.BubbleJuggler.com
E-mail: geoffakins@hotmail.com

Author and CEO, OneCoach
The Answer: Grow Any Business, Achieve Financial Freedom, and Live an Extraordinary Life

Telephone: 858-792-1250
Web site www.ReadTheAnswer.com
E-mail: Info@OneCoach.com

Judee is a real estate broker, author and self-described, lifelong learner. She wrote *Drama is Optional: A Guide for Teens* after more than 20 years of studying with many great teachers in the field of self-improvement and learning firsthand how to use the principles described in her book. Her passion is to help make a difference in the lives of teenagers—giving them the tools they need to know "who they are" and allowing them to wake up to their magnificence within.

Telephone: 530-432-5639
Web site: www.dramaisoptional.com
E-mail: judee@judeeausnow.com

Beard, Lee *225*
Lee is a television producer, advertising executive and business developer. He lives in Arkansas when not traveling as the co-creator of the *Wake Up...Live the Life You Love* book series. Lee is an author featured in more than a dozen motivational and inspirational volumes. He concentrates on bringing the power of the Wake Up network to bear on the challenges of business development. If you've had a "wake up" moment you would like to share, visit wakeupmoment.com to tell your story!

Web site: www.wakeupmoment.com, www.wakeuplive.net, leebeard.com
E-mail: lee@wakeuplive.net

Beckwith, Dr. Michael *129*
Founder and Spiritual Director

Agape International Spiritual Center
Address: Culver City, CA
Web site: www.agapelive.com

Bertozzini, Emanuela *87*
Emanuela Bertozzini has practiced in Italy for more than 10 years after living and practicing abroad. She has been trained as a Louise Hay teacher, spent two years at the Barbara Brennan school of healing and was trained by Brian Weiss as a past life therapist. She firmly believes in the power of energy and love and her practice reflects her beliefs.

Address: Roma, Italy
Via dei Gracchi 278 00192
Telephone: 0039 3392122833

Bilger, Lora M. Dipl. Päd *147*
Lora obtained her Ph.D. comparable degree from the University of Tuebingen, Germany. Since 1983, she has been a practicing psychologist, psychotherapist, body work, team supervisor and life and business coach. She was also trained as a physiotherapist and in EFT and she works internationally. She also has been working for an international organization nationally and internationally for more than fifteen years. Lora has developed AHA-Work and AHA-Therapie® and speaks English and German.

Skype-name: blessedskyblue
To contact her at Skype use code: "AHA-Work"
Telephone: 0049-0170-9323395 (observe time differences to Germany)
Web site: www.Know-What-Is-Love.com

After more than 25 years as an executive in the healthcare industry, Tom developed an executive leadership and organizational transformation coaching practice named The XLR8 Team in 1994 and serves as its president and head coach. He is most grateful to his anchor client, Wegmans Food Markets, currently in the Hall of Fame in *Fortune* magazine's "100 Best Companies to Work For®" list, reaching No. 1 overall in 2005.

Address: The XLR8 Team, Inc., 279 Totem Trail,
Rochester, NY 14617
Telephone: 585-544-1570
Web site: www.thexlr8team.com
E-mail: tbrady@thexlr8team.com

Nicole is a master fitness instructor, renowned coach and the CEO and founder of "Artistry In Motion" A.I.M. For Excellence, Inc. Nicole is one of the most sought-after motivational speakers, writers and teachers across the globe today. She guides clients in the "art" of wellness, health, vitality, physical transformation and physical regeneration. Nicole rides horses, sails boats, does acrobatics, figure skates, dances and empowers others by helping people be pain-free and by teaching the power of the body. Nicole inspires the beauty and the glory of the human form, which she coins "Artistry In Motion," which of course, is the way she lives.

Suzi has owned and operated successful businesses for over 25 years and has dedicated her life to learning about personal effectiveness, business start-ups/operations and management. Suzi is an inspired speaker whose passion is in connecting with and guiding others to use the power of their minds and hearts to realize their dreams.

Brian Tracy Focal Point Coach
Address: 8435 Lake Park Trl
Helena, MT 59602
Telephone: 406-443-3176 or 406-422-0937
E-mail: sbroadw1@aol.com

Dr. Buttar is trained in surgery, ER medicine and served as brigade surgeon and ER director while in the U.S. Army. He is board certified in clinical metal toxicology, has achieved fellowship status in three separate medical societies and is the medical director at the Center for Advanced Medicine and Clinical Research™, treating patients who are unresponsive to conventional treatments such as cancer and autism. He's ranked among the Top 50 Doctors in the U.S. since 2003 by Phillips Publishing and Dr. Steve Sinatra.

Address: 9630 Julian Clark Ave.
Huntersville, NC 28078
Telephone: 704-895-WELL (9355)
Web sites: www.DrButtar.com, www.TheMedicalSeries.com, www.TransD.com

Dr. Cole began life in Kentucky and has yet to fully recover from it. He was driven to get degrees in medicine and psychology in attempts to find life's meaning. He now spends his professional days practicing medicine, writing, developing therapies, and consulting. On the personal side, he enjoys good drink, good food, good company, good music, good movies, and a good life.

E-mail: info@colecenter.com

   Margit is an energy and life coach and motivational speaker. Coaching clients from all around the world, she helps people build their confidence, find direction and live full lives using energy vibration principles.

Energy and Life Coach & Motivational Speaker
Address: Noosa, QLD, Australia
Telephone: +61 7 407 532 722
E-mail: fearlessliving@live.com

   Melinda has more than 25 years experience in senior and executive corporate management. A CPA by profession—not by personality—Melinda is a prosperity expert, speaker, trainer and coach. She is the founder and CEO of T-Zone Consulting, Inc., in the Texas Hill Country, whose goal is to help individuals and businesses achieve greater prosperity by teaching them to break boundaries that are limiting their success.

T-Zone Consulting, Inc.
Address: 24165 IH 10 West, Ste. 217-476
San Antonio, TX 78257-1159
E-mail: Melinda@TZoneConsulting.com

   Shelley Berger Dooley, P.M.H.N.P., is a Psychiatric Nurse Practitioner, providing psychiatric evaluations, brief therapy and medication management for adults. Melanie R. Schockett, Ph.D., is a licensed psychologist providing individual, couple and family counseling to adults and adolescents. They are both in private practice in Scottsdale, Arizona. Together, they have over 60 years of experience in the field of mental health.

Address: Scottsdale Psychological Associates 11000 N. Scottsdale Road, #163
Scottsdale, Arizona 85254
Telephone: 480-922-5440 Fax: 480 922-5445
Web sites: www.boomersinthebedroom.com, www.scottsdalepsych.com
E-mail: Boomersinthebedroom@yahoo.com

Brett trained at the Palmer College of Chiropractic, graduating in 1977. He has since been practicing in Auckland, New Zealand.

Epsom Center for Spinal Health
Address: 128 Manukau Rd.
Epsom Auckland, New Zealand
E-mail: bret@ihug.co.nz

Best-selling author and lecturer.
Wayne is the author of these best-selling books: *Power of Intention, Real Magic, Manifesting Your Destiny* and *Pulling Your Own Strings.*

Peter is an author, speaker and mentor who is passionate about helping people discover their true power. His book, *Lighten Your Load*, endorsed by stars from the hit movie *The Secret*, is testimony to the fact that it is never too late to do what you really love to do.

Web site: www.peterfield.co.uk
E-mail: peter@peterfield.co.uk

A natural health advocate and Living Food chef and teacher, she has earned a reputation for delivering sharp and definitive up-to-the-minute lifestyle change information. Both passionate and energetic about her work, Sharynne has been able to help hundreds of people learn how to make small changes in lifestyle behavior that add up to big changes in their health and overall wellness. With more than 30 years in the medical field, she brings a refreshing approach to change that one can live with for life!

Telephone: 888-331-3236
Web sites: www.FreshFusionLive.tv

A sought-after speaker, author and workshop leader, Bill Harris is founder and director of Centerpointe Research Institute and creator of Holosync® audio technology. Started in 1989 with borrowed recording equipment set up on his kitchen table, Centerpointe now has over 150,000 Holosync® users in 172 countries.

Centerpointe Research Institute
Address: 1700 NW 167th Pl., Suite 220
Beaverton, OR 97006
Telephone: 800-945-2741
Web site: www.centerpointe.com

John Herbert is a retired electrician. He spent 25 years of his life as a minister, becoming very familiar with many religions and philosophies of the world. In 1984 he realized that religion, with much of its confusing dogma, was not bettering his relationship with God. He quit religion and continued his search for the truth. He has had many wonderful experiences since then, and would like to share them with you.

Address: 12523, 25th Court East
Parrish, FL 34219
Telephone: 941-531-7187
Web site: Under construction
E-mail: civilization1@mac.com

Ian is a co-author of *Wake Up...Live the Life You Love*, author of *University of Life—351 Insights to Inspire Happiness* at UniversityofLife.com and "21 Internet Marketing Myths Dispelled" at WebsiteHeaven.com.au.

Address: Perth, Western Australia
Web sites: WebsiteHeaven.com.au, UniversityofLife.com
E-mail: language@gol.com

Ernie is currently acting and writing for TV and film and is available for speaking and personal appearances. Ernie has performed in various TV shows, movies and plays, including *Taxi, OZ, Ghost Busters, The Hand that Rocks the Cradle, Congo, Miss Congeniality, The Crow* and a variety of others. He has also written two published plays, *Rebellion 369* and *My Kingdom Come*, and is working on others in the near future. His personal representative, Thomas Cushing, can be contacted at Innovative Artist, 310-656-0400, and Ernie can be reached through his Web site.

Web site: www.Ernie-Hudson.com.

Guy's vision is to create an online global community to support each other's personal development and growth and to do good in the world. Guy is the founder of championsclubcommunity.com, which seeks to support and profile everyday real life champions, people whose unassuming actions are a source of inspiration and motivation to others. Guy's organization is a UK partner of the world famous Franklin Covey® organization, founded by Stephen R. Covey, author of the *7 Habits of Highly Effective People*.

Telephone: 0044 (0)1702 433508
Web site: http://championsclubcommunity.com
E-mail: guy.insull@championsclubcommunity.com

At 32 years old, Laura has a degree in law and a master's degree in journalism and communication. She's a freelance photographer, artist, art dealer, web designer and business consultant. She loves tennis, golf and diving. She always wants to know more and now attends philosophy classes at an Italian university.

Web sites: www.laurajelenkovich.com, laurajelenkovich@fastwebnet.it, myspace:jele
E-mail: superjele@hotmail.com

Rogeema is an electrical engineer by profession. She is also an ardent karate-ka and is currently at the level of 2nd dan black belt. Her true passion is developing people and helping them reach their full potential through business, sport, spirituality, personal development and education. She is also active in her community as a human rights activist and serves on the Western Cape committee of Mensa as the editor of The Tablet (quarterly e-zine).

Address: P.O. Box 24290, Lansdowne, 7779
Cape Town, South Africa
Telephone: +27 (0)72 482 9018
Web site: www.RogeemaKenny.com
E-mail: info@rogeemakenny.com

At the early age of six, Zachary began acting, singing and dancing in school and local theater productions. He has performed in regional roles such as *Grease, The Outsiders, Oliver, The Wizard of Oz* and *Big River*. But, it was his portrayal of Jesus in Ojai's *Godspell* that brought him to the attention of Hollywood. He completed a supporting role in the television movie *Big Shot: Confessions of a Campus Bookie* (2002) (TV). He then began acting as Kipp Steadman in the TV series *Less Than Perfect* (2002) and was also seen in the television movie *See Jane Date* (2003) (TV) on the WB. He also stars in NBC's *Chuck*. In his spare time, Zachary enjoys skateboarding, snowboarding, skydiving and participating in various other sports (Bio information obtained from www.IMDB.com).

Since 1991, Alex Mandossian has generated over $233 million in sales and profits for his clients and partners using electronic marketing media such as TV infomercials, online catalogs, 24-hour recorded messages, voice/fax broadcasting, teleseminars, webinars, podcasts and internet marketing. He is the CEO of Heritage House Publishing, Inc., a boutique electronic marketing and publishing company. He lives in San Francisco with his wife, Aimee, and children, Gabriel and Breanna.

Web site: www.AlexMandossian.com

Michelle McConville is a freelance writer. She is a member of Work at Home Project Zone, Rise to Success and Sharing Zero Point. Michelle earned her PMP from the Project Management Institute. She has been running her own business since 2007 and currently lives in Las Vegas with her two dogs. When not coaching others to becoming more satisfied with life she enjoys a daily gratitude walk with her dogs and spending time with her two adult children.

Telephone: 702-243-8062
Web sites: www.100poundsless.com, www.michellemcconville.com

Dr. Anand Menon is the founder and leader of Life in the Word ministries and Anand Menon International. Anand is a life transformational coach, management development expert, a motivational speaker and an inspirational teacher who speaks internationally at business and community seminars and conventions. He has recorded over 440 teachings and has helped thousands discover their true potential.

Life in the Word
Telephone: 0097143552780 Mobile: 00971506004069
Web sites: www.lifeintheword.me, www.anandmenon.org
E-mail: anand@lifeintheword.me, anandmenon@windowslive.com

For over 15 years, Kate has been working with business leaders to help them create the company they envision and reap the rewards. She empowers entrepreneurs to build bold and fulfilling companies and keep more of the money they make. Her approach is hands-on, insightful, practical and humorous. She is a sought after public speaker, author, and coach, and lives with her family in Massachusetts.

Business Concepts, Inc.
Telephone: 508-281-6486
Web site: www.business-concepts.biz
E-mail: khm@business-concepts.biz

Cecilia Nannini is a personal empowerment mentor, life coach, internationally published author and the mother of a beautiful girl. Her love and passion is to inspire and empower others to create the life they desire. Her approach is to share the powerful secrets and techniques that have made such an impact in her life. Visit her Web site for a free special report, "Top 10 Powerful Secrets to Empower Your Life," or register to receive information from free tele-seminars offered to help you live the life you love.

Web site: www.PowerfulSecrets.com
E-mail: cecilia@powerfulsecrets.com

Michal is passionate about helping people discover and live to their full potential. She believes that a seed of greatness resides in everyone.
Empowerment coach, Reiki master/teacher, hypnotherapist, past life regressionist

Telephone: 267-722-8281, 215-200-5762
Web site: www.mindurmind.com
E-mail: michal@mindurmind.com

Pampling, Danielle *189*

Danielle Pampling is an expert at turning potential into superior performance and positive results. Danielle is a passionate, inspiring speaker and trainer who has been featured on Australian radio and television programs. Danielle's vision for empowering others to live a life they love has moved her to write and share her experiences. Devoted wife and mother of three, Danielle calls beautiful Perth, Australia her home.

Address: Perth, Western Australia
Telephone: 0011 61 413 766 808
Web site: www.transformers.acnrep.com
E-mail: transformers@myacn.net.au

Pitts, Joy *161*

Joy Pitts was born in Indiana, has three children and loves living in Hawaii. Her interests include quantum physics, metaphysics, the paranormal, universal laws, time travel, worm holes, and black holes. She spends time training her mind, meditating and facilitating "A Course in Miracles." She also enjoys working with young people, motivating them and assisting them in transforming them into happy, healthy and whole young adults.

Porter, Joy *217*

Joy owns a successful direct sales company near Philadelphia, PA. When she's not selling, she's sharing how being in sales can be a tool for personal growth as it has been in her life. Her latest offering reveals a process to help sales people remove fears and resentments that may be holding them back in their career and life. For details you can visit her Web site.

Address: P.O. Box 204
Colmar, PA 18915
Telephone: 267-337-3145
Web site: www.SalesForPersonalGrowth.com
E-mail: Info@SalesForPersonalGrowth.com

Pounder, Jana *19*

Ms. Pounder used her background in education and her personal experience as a single parent to establish a relocation-destination services company. Jana's mission is to help an individual or family re-create a lifestyle and make invaluable connections to their new community.

Talent Bank Relocation, LLC
Address: Phoenix, Arizona
Web site: www.TalentBankRelocation.com
E-mail: JanaPounder@TalentBankRelocation.com

Rav-Hon, Orna *57*
Orna Rav-Hon is a well-known Israeli poet who has published four books and has received literary prizes. She believes in the ability of every person to take control of their life and in the responsibility of every person to change the world for the best with the gifts that the Creator gave them. She uses her gift of writing as a means of bringing people closer together and to restore peace in human hearts.

Address: Hailanot 4 Cfar-Sirkin
49935 Israel
Telephone: 972-3-9327475 Cell: 972-523-633498
Web site: www.tasteofisrael.org, Enter "Orna Rav-Hon" in the search box.
E-mail: ornarav@zahav.net.il

Reid, Gregory Scott *141*
A #1 best-selling author, Gregory Scott Reid has become known for his energy and candor on the speaker's platform and his signature phrase "Always Good!" An experienced entrepreneur in his own right, he has become known as an effective leader, coach, and "The Millionaire Mentor."

Web site: www.AlwaysGood.com

Robertson, Pam, Ph.D. *143*
Pam loves exploring the beaches in Nova Scotia, Canada and is an avid bird watcher. She writes and speaks professionally about careers, training and facilitation and is backed by a Ph.D. in career development and stints in a range of industries, including six years in the military. Pam has launched her first novel written under the name, Maggie Bendar, and has posted a blog where she welcomes your visit and comments.

Address: P.O. Box 244
Lower Sackville, NS B4C 2S9
Telephone: 902-222-9212
Email: pam@pamrobertson.org
Web site: http://andthebandplayedonmylawn.blogspot.com

Rodriguez, Edward A. *63*
Edward is better known as "Mr. In-Power." He has created unique behavioral-change-technologies that have positioned him as one of the most respected Latino Motivational and Transformational Trainers. He is the founder and CEO of the In-Powerment Center, an executive coach and author. He also writes a monthly newsletter, *In-Podérate!*, which reaches more than 9,000 subscribers worldwide. In English or Spanish, Edward helps his clients and audiences around the world to attain the breakthroughs that enable them to accomplish desired results in both their personal and professional lives.

Telephone: 1-888-2-IN-POWER (in the US), 1-718-543-8831 (worldwide)
Web site: www.EdwardRodriguez.com
E-mail: info@EdwardRodriguez.com

Monika Summerfield is a psychotherapist, yoga teacher and a healer. She is the former executive director and cofounder of the Diamond Counseling Center. She has helped numerous people overcome depression, trauma and relationship challenges and has empowered them to live with strength and open their hearts in the directions of their dreams. She has a practice in Huntington Beach, California.

Address: 16052 Beach Blvd., Ste 212
Huntington Beach, CA 92647
Telephone: 714-745-3238
Web site: www.monikasummerfield.com
E-mail: monika@monikasummerfield.com

Peter Thurin is one of Australia's most experienced and successful public speakers and facilitators, working with corporations and individuals around the world through his company, Blackbelt in Excellence. Peter has presented in Australia, Europe, Asia Pacific and the U.S. He holds a black belt in Tae Kwon Do and uses martial arts principles as the basis for his performance enhancement corporate work.

Address: Blackbelt in Excellence P.O. Box 392
Toorak, VIC 3142, Australia
Telephone: +61 (0)407 568 416
Web-site: www.blackbeltinexcellence.com.au
E-mail: prt@blackbeltinexcellence.com.au

Brian Tracy is the most listened to audio author on personal and business success in the world today. His fast-moving talks and seminars on leadership, sales, managerial effectiveness and business strategy are loaded with powerful, proven ideas and strategies that people can immediately apply to get better results in every area.

Brian Tracy International
Address: 462 Stevens Ave., Suite 202
Solana Beach, CA 92075
Telephone: 858-436-7300
Web site: www.BrianTracy.com
E-mail: BrianTracy@briantracy.com

Michelle Tweedie is a holistic life coach and author of the e-book *The Silent Sufferers*. Michelle lives in New Zealand with her partner of 10 years, Bryan. She is a mother of two teenage children and a caregiver for an 18 year-old. Michelle was plagued with migraines and headaches for 26 years. Driven by her own desire and persistence, Michelle spent years doing research to break the cycle. Her passion is now to help free others of migraines and headaches.

Web site: www.empower2health.com

Connie Peterson Uthoff is a martial artist residing in Maryland with her two children, Taylor and Kerrie (also black belts). She is the recipient of a 2006 Maryland Businesswoman of the Year award, a Congressional Medal of Distinction and a National Leadership Award. Born in Germany, she has her B.A. from St. Olaf College and plans to complete her master's degree in strategic intelligence by 2010.

Telephone: 301-675-9905
Web site: www.TKManagement.net
E-mail: cuinia@aol.com

Mr. Van Praag has been a marketing and business counselor to national advertising and procurement managers for the past 30 years. Ray has grown up in the ad production business. His corporation, Ernst-Van Praag, Inc., specializes in Insight Marketing, which helps sustain communication and simplifies marketing strategies for many of the world's largest advertisers.

Ernst-Van Praag, Inc.
Address: 4800 N. Federal Highway Ste E 207
Boca Raton, FL 33431
Telephone: 561-447-0557
E-mail: evpray@aol.com

She began acting at the age of nine (portraying Oliver in the musical of the same name) and continued to work extensively on the stage, performing in over 50 plays at regional and professional theaters in the Tampa Bay area. Liz has appeared as a regular or recurring character on nine television shows including *CSI, The Tick, Maximum Bob, Brotherly Love* and *All My Children* (for which she was nominated for a Daytime Emmy). Her hobbies are writing (she has sold two potential pilot scripts to studios), scuba diving and running (Bio information obtained from www.IMBD.com).

Venu is an author and educator in behavior modification. She is presently developing an interactive computer program, Time Out®, through her non-profit company, Time Out, Inc. The mission of Time Out, Inc. is, "To elevate humanity's ability to take personal responsibility."

Web sites: www.empowered.cc • www.healthy.net/rainbowstress • www.timeout.org
E-mail: venu@timeout.org

Charlinda (Charlie) enjoys sharing her knowledge as a speaker and is available for speaking engagements. She has spoken on how to take control of your finances for women and is a co-author in *Wake Up...Live the Life You Love*. She is a television writer, producer and the host of *Forever Alive* and *CFB Awareness*. She has also written newspaper articles for the *Pembroke Advertiser News* and has over 20 years experience in helping people. Coming from a small town in Ontario, she received inspiration and acquired the knowledge to help others. Her grandfather helped her more than he knew by telling her constantly in her formative years to, "Learn something new every day and you will never die!" She now lives in the large city of Calgary, Alberta and loves it. She continues to grow thanks to his advice and everyone who helped her on the way.

Heidi Wright's first career was as an officer for the California Highway Patrol. After 13 years with the CHP, she retired due to injury. She then studied metaphysics and meditation. She became a professional animal communicator, is featured in a best-selling book and appeared on a hit TV show in Japan. She does consultations/readings, teaches workshops and writes for animal rights.

Address: P.O. Box 482
Malin, OR 97632
Web site: www.CritterConnections.net

Dr. David Yeh woke up to become more than just a follower. Instead, he became the trailblazer on a path that led him to a life he loves.

Telephone: 630-527-2877
Web sites: www.wayofyeh.com, www.edward.org
E-mail: davidmyyeh@yahoo.com

Wake Up...
Live the Life You Love

Empowered

Resources

RESOURCES

Brian Tracy International
462 Stevens Ave, Suite 202
Solana Beach, CA 92075
858-481-2977

Brian Tracy International offers three services: Brian Tracy Online, Brian Tracy University and Brian Tracy Speaking. Brian Tracy Online provides learning programs and educational materials to ensure success in the subjects of entrepreneurship, finance, management, personal development, sales, and time management. You will find an array of programs in CD, DVD and book format to assist in the development of your personal greatness. Visit the web site at www.BrianTracy.com or call the customer service representatives at 858-481-2977. They are happy to discuss your personal needs and areas of focus to ensure the perfect learning program is selected.

Brian Tracy University is the perfect choice for students who are ambitious, persistent, self-reliant, disciplined, responsible, focused, committed to continuous learning and growth, as well as determined to increase their income and profits. Once you enroll in Brian Tracy University, Brian will teach you how to increase your sales and income, improve your revenues, cash flow and profits as well as how to become an excellent manager and leader, while boosting your personal productivity and performance. Brian has successfully helped thousands of people reach their personal and financial goals. Allow Brian Tracy to help you achieve these same goals by enrolling today! To speak with the National Enrollment Director, please call 858-481-2977.

Brian Tracy Speaking offers fast-moving, informative, enjoyable and entertaining presentations. Brian has a wonderful ability to customize each talk for his particular audience. He presents a series of great ideas and strategies with a rare combination of fact, humor, insights and practical concepts that audience members can apply immediately to get better results. To book a speaking event, please call Victor Risling at 858-481-2977.

RESOURCES

Centerpointe Research Institute
1700 NW 167th Place, Suite 220
Beaverton, OR 97006
800-945-2741

Centerpointe Research Institute offers two programs, The Holosync Solution and The Life Principles Integration Process. The Holosync Solution uses Centerpointe's proprietary Holosync audio technology to place the listener in states of deep meditation, creating dramatic and rapid changes in mental, emotional and spiritual health. Over 150,000 people in 172 countries have used Holosync to improve their lives. By filling out a short survey at www.centerpointe.com you can get a free Holosync demo CD and a Special Report about Holosync and how it works, or call 800-945-2741.

In Centerpointe's Life Principles Integration Process, you'll learn the internal processes you use to unconsciously and automatically create your internal and external results, and how to take control of this process so you can consciously and intentionally create the internal and external results you really want. For more information about The Life Principles Integration Process, and to hear a free preview lesson, visit www.centerpointe.com

RESOURCES

Alex Mandossian
www.AlexMandossian.com

Since 1991, Alex Mandossian has generated over $233 million in sales and profits for his clients and partners via "electronic marketing" media such as TV Infomercials, online catalogs, 24-hour recorded messages, voice/fax broadcasting, teleseminars, webinars, podcasts and Internet marketing. To get the full story, visit this web page: www.TeleseminarETR.com.

Alex has personally consulted Dale Carnegie® Training, New York University, 1ShoppingCart Corp, Mutuals.com, Nightingale-Conant, The Strategic Coach®, Super Camp®, Trim Spa™ and others.

He has hosted teleseminars with many of the world's top Thought Leaders such as Mark Victor Hansen, Jack Canfield, Stephen Covey, Les Brown, David Allen, Vic Conant, Brian Tracy, David Bach, Harvey Mackay, Robert Cialdini, T. Harv Eker, Lisa Nichols, Michael Masterson, Joe Vitale, Loral Langemeier, Bob Proctor, Michael Gerber, Jay Abraham, Donald Trump and many others.

He has trained over 13,300 teleseminar students since 2001 and claims that practically any entrepreneur can transform their annual income into a weekly income once they apply his principle-centered electronic marketing strategies. KEY POINT: Alex's 2001 annual income became an hourly income by 2006 (sixteen times) while tripling his days off!

Alex lives in the San Francisco Bay Area with his wife, Aimee and his two children, Gabriel and Breanna. He enjoys over 90 "Free Days" each year, all made possible due to the power of his teleseminar marketing businesses.

Wake Up...
Live the Life You Love

Empowered

Noetic Pyramid

Noetic Pyramid

The Noetic (no-EH-tik) Pyramid is a systemic way of looking at the benefits of learning and implementing the attitudes, beliefs and behaviors that must always precede real abundance in life.

NOESIS (no-ë´-sis, noun) [Greek. To perceive] 1. Philosophical: Purely intellectual apprehension. 2. Psychological: Cognition, especially through direct and self-evident knowledge. Noetic (adjective).

There is a way to know; therefore, there is a way to know what to do in life. The answers are not concealed from us, but are available through noesis: a purely intellectual process which gives us sure answers, if only we will look and grasp what we see.

But no one can see—or even look with energy and purpose—unless the mind is clear and the attention is directed. We need a guiding principle that gives us a direction and a foundation.

Building on what they have discovered over years of working with teachers, mentors, motivators, philosophers, psychologists and business leaders, Steven E and Lee Beard have devised the Noetic Pyramid: a structure of beliefs and learning that takes us from the firmest of foundations to the kind of life we can most enjoy; the kind of life which can most benefit those around us; the kind of life that may change the world.

Foundations
With your firm faith in God, you have the proper perspective to process all instructions that you receive. Then, when you give adequate attention to your health, you have a solid foundation to allow you to learn and utilize what we call The 7 Secrets of Living the Life You Love.

Charting the Course
Then we must develop the internal structures of abundance: find your purpose through meditation or prayer, then visualize your desired future. To embark on this process without a firm grounding in belief and without the physical tools to support your mind and spirit, you are almost sure to be disappointed.

Reach Out to Expand the Possibilities
The Pyramid then leads you from a firm foundation to the external techniques of planning, teamwork, marketing and acquiring the necessary money. None of these external elements will be meaningful without the foundational elements, but neither will these essential elements inherently lead to abundance.

Abundance and Gratitude
We must realize the benefits of learning and utilize the internal structure and external techniques to create abundance, freedom, gratitude and fulfillment so we can truly live the life we love. An abundant life has meaning beyond ourselves, so we must seek to improve the lives of others. When we use our freedom to the benefit of others, when we are thankful for the opportunity to share the blessings of a materially abundant life, then we are fulfilled beyond our ability to imagine.

This is what we want everyone around the world to do: *Wake Up...Live the Life You Love.*

Wake Up...
Live the Life You Love

Empowered

A Gift For You

Wake Up...Live the Life You Love wants to give you a gift that will get you moving on the path to personal abundance. Please visit www.wakeupgift.com today!